The Strengths Toolbox

For a complete list of Management Books 2000 titles
visit our web-site on http://www.mb2000.com

The Strengths Toolbox

*All the tools you need
to build and develop
strengths in the workplace*

Mike Pegg

2000

Copyright © Mike Pegg 2008

All rights reserved. No part of this publication may be reproduced, stored in a retrieval system, or transmitted in any form or by any means, electronic, mechanical, photocopying, recording, or otherwise without the prior permission of the publishers.

First published in 2006 by Management Books 2000 Ltd
Forge House, Limes Road
Kemble, Cirencester
Gloucestershire, GL7 6AD, UK
Tel: 0044 (0) 1285 771441
Fax: 0044 (0) 1285 771055
Email: info@mb2000.com
Web: www.mb2000.com

This book is sold subject to the condition that it shall not, by way of trade or otherwise, be lent, resold, hired out, or otherwise circulated without the publisher's prior consent in any form of binding or cover other than that in which it is published and without a similar condition including this condition being imposed upon the subsequent purchaser.

British Library Cataloguing in Publication Data is available

Produced by Digital Book Print Ltd

ISBN 9781852525736

Introduction

Welcome to *The Strengths Toolbox*. This book provides practical tools that you can use to continue to achieve peak performance. It offers a series of '3 tips' on each of the following themes:

- Strengths – how to build on your strengths;
- Super teams – how to build super teams;
- Sharing knowledge – how to pass on your knowledge to help other people to succeed.

The toolbox aims to be practical – so each piece is written in a relatively 'simple' way. Obviously much more could be written about the philosophy and principles behind each tool. You can discover more about the background in books such as *The Strengths Way, Strengths Coaching in 90 Minutes* and *The Art of Mentoring.*

Pick and mix your way through the book. Dip in anywhere and see if there is a tool you can use. The ideas are grouped under strengths, super teams and sharing knowledge, but there are many overlaps. So, as ever, 'take the best and leave the rest'. Use the tools in your own way to practise the art of building on strengths.

Contents

Introduction	5
Strengths	11

3 tips for:

building on your strengths	12
being in your element	17
recognising where you go 'a, b ____ then leap to ____ z'	20
employing your personal radar	24
following your successful style	27
clarifying your perfect role	31
understanding your 'solid ground' and 'dangerous ground'	35
clarifying your perfect customer	38
reaching out to potential sponsors	42
making clear contracts with sponsors	46
managing sponsors by focusing on the '3 Rs'	50
being of 'high value & hard to replace'	53
balancing the great work and grunt work	57
practising the art of mental rehearsal	60
being able to flow – rather than freeze	63
being real in your role	67
finishing	69
managing crises successfully	73
recognising that 'what you focus on, you become'	77
making good use of the fallow times	81
getting positive energy	84
getting a 'perfect ten'	87
surfing the sigmoid curve	90
spring-cleaning your life	93
creating perfect days	96

The Strengths Toolbox

Super teams   **99**

3 tips for:

building a super team	100
clarifying your team's picture of perfection	104
clarifying your team's strategies for success	107
building a team based on 'similarity of spirit' & 'diversity of strengths'	110
getting the right balance of 'soul players' and 'star players'	114
getting the right balance of decision-makers, drivers & deliverers	118
making a clear contract with your team	122
knowing when to 'debate, decide, deliver'	125
clarifying each person's contribution to the picture of perfection	129
co-ordinating your team's strengths	132
communicating your leadership style to people	135
communicating the results, rules and rewards	141
balancing being an energiser, educator and enforcer	144
following the STAGE model of leadership	147
being a good co-ordinator	151
balancing consistency and creativity in a team	155
'rewarding the behaviour you want repeated'	159
creating momentum by changing the physical things	163
encouraging a person to work towards the picture of perfection	167
making sure somebody completes a mission	171
being true to yourself – even if you get sacked	174
building on the positive energy in an organisation	178
shifting a culture by building successful prototypes	181
inviting your team to answer the 'rolling contract' question	186
communicating your team's story	189

Contents

Sharing knowledge — 197

3 tips for:

clarifying what you can offer as a mentor	198
facilitating a mentoring session	201
establishing a coaching contract	207
being a good encourager	211
building on a person's strengths	216
clarifying a person's will to reach their goal	220
clarifying the goals for a development session	224
understanding the picture inside someone's head	227
employing the 'second empathy'	231
using the three keywords 'what, how, when'	235
educating people by focusing on the 3 Is	239
running an enjoyable and effective educational session	242
moving between the concept and the concrete	245
communicating with 'architects', 'builders' and 'craftsmen'	249
educating people to 'see' things in a professional situation	252
understanding change on the primary and secondary levels	257
producing great design	260
understanding the 'second simplicity'	264
finding 'win-win' solutions	267
running a super teams workshop	273

Strengths

3 tips for building on your strengths

Everybody has strengths – activities in which they deliver 'As', rather than 'Bs' or 'Cs'. So let's consider what you do best and, if you wish, get feedback from people who you respect. You can then focus on how to create the opportunity to use your talents. Sometimes this will be in your personal life, sometimes in your professional life. Let's explore how to take these steps.

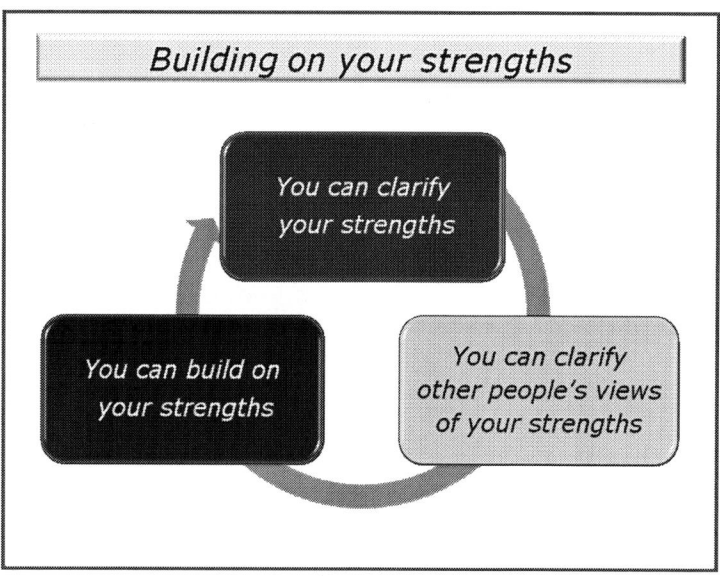

1) *You can clarify your strengths.*

Begin by tackling the exercise called *My strengths*. Start by describing the activities where you deliver 'As', 'Bs' and 'Cs'. Be as specific as possible when highlighting your top talents. You may start by saying, for example, "I am good at leading teams." Try to be more concrete. You may do your best work with teams that are driving a pioneering project; making the 'new rules' in their field; consist of positive people; enjoy lots of autonomy – providing they deliver; must

Strengths

hit a deadline or whatever. Here are some guidelines regarding when you deliver 'As', 'Bs' or 'Cs'.

Your 'As'.   These are the specific activities where:

You feel in your element – you are at ease and yet excel. You are calm, clear and deliver concrete results. You see the destination quickly. You go 'a, b – then leap to – z'. You see patterns quickly. You have an almost photographic memory. You make complicated things simple. You have a good track record of finishing. You get feedback from people you respect that you score at least 8/10.

Your 'Bs'.   These are the activities where either:

You may have the potential to deliver 'As', but aren't doing so at the moment. You were once able to perform the task to a high standard, but now you get bored. You can perform the task to a reasonable standard, but will never hit the heights.

Your 'Cs'.   These are the activities where either:

You simply have no 'feeling' for the activity. You keep making fundamental mistakes. You have no interest or desire to learn.

My strengths

'As'. The specific activities where I deliver 'As' are:

* ....

* ....

* ....

'Bs'. The specific activities where I deliver 'Bs' are:

* ....

* ....

The Strengths Toolbox

'Cs'. *The specific activities where I deliver 'Cs' are:*

* ....

2) You can clarify other people's views of your strengths.

Choose two or three people *who you respect*. Ask if they would be willing to do the exercise called *Strengths feedback from other people*. If so, invite them to describe three things. First, the specific activities in which they believe you deliver 'As' – plus their reasons for listing these things. Second, the activities in which they believe you could potentially deliver 'As' – plus their reasons. Third, the steps they believe you can take to build on your strengths.

This exercise can provide a good reality check – but two points are worth mentioning. a) Choose people you respect – it is not 360 feedback. Why? Peak performers are extremists – they do some things extremely well and are not always appreciated by everybody. That does not mean they should dilute their talent, however, to be more 'middle of the road'. b) Ask people to be honest and, if possible, super-specific when they give feedback. Collect their views, ask questions if you would like more information, then move onto the next step.

Strengths feedback from other people

'As'. *The specific activities where I believe the person delivers 'As' are:*

* ....

* ....

The reasons why I have listed these activities are:

* ....

* ....

Potential 'As'. *The activities where I believe the person could potentially deliver 'As' are:*

* ....

* ....

The reasons why I believe the person could deliver 'As' in these activities are:

* ....

* ....

Building on strengths. *The specific things I believe the person can do to build on their strengths are:*

* ....

* ....

3) *You can build on your strengths.*

"We do this exercise with all our employees to build up a real 'strengths profile,'" said the MD of one company. "Every good sports coach knows the specific talents of their athletes. They know these in detail – rather than relying on general statements – but few organisations go to such lengths. The strengths profile we create goes far beyond normal psychometric tests. We know each person's top talents and how to use these when it matters."

Looking at the information you have gathered, take time out to reflect and do some in-depth work. First, describe how you can build on where you deliver 'As'. Second, describe how you can manage the consequences of your 'Bs' & 'Cs'. Third, bearing in mind your 'A' talents, describe what you believe would be your best contribution to an employer. Try completing the following sentences.

The Strengths Toolbox

'As'. The things I can do to build on my 'As' are:

* ....

* ....

* ....

'Bs' & 'Cs'. The things I can do to manage the consequences of my 'Bs' & 'Cs' are:

* ....

* ....

Bearing in mind these answers, I believe my best contribution to an employer would be:

* ....

This is just a beginning. After clarifying your strengths, set specific goals and work hard to achieve success. You can then continue to build on your own – and other people's – 'A' talents.

3 tips for being in your element

"They were in their element," is a phrase often used to describe somebody in top form. For example, a professor gives an inspiring lecture, a dancer produces a marvellous performance or a chef creates a wonderful meal. Look for the specific activities in which you feel at ease and yet excel. Here are three tips for focusing on where this happens for you.

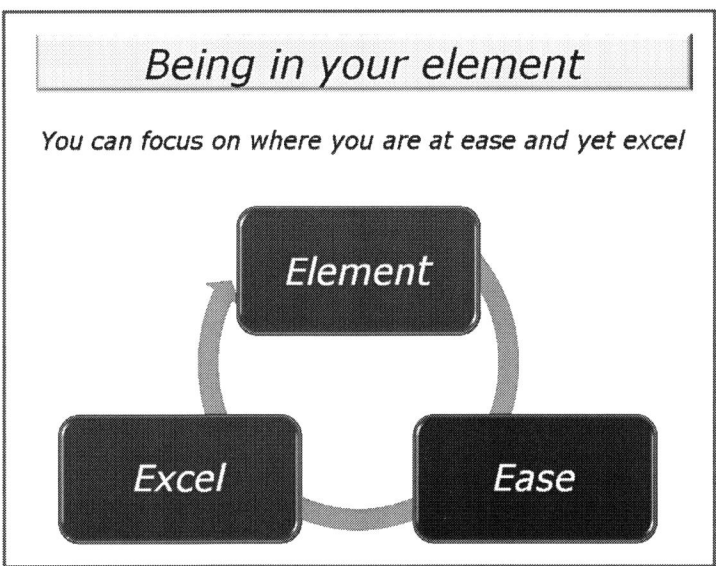

1) You can clarify when you are in your element.

One IT worker said: "I really enjoy solving seemingly impossible computer problems. Everybody else is going crazy – saying how much money the customer is losing – but I feel calm during the crisis. My company now employs me as a full-time trouble-shooter to work on-site with clients." Try tackling the exercise on this theme. Describe the situations in which you feel at ease and yet excel.

The Strengths Toolbox

The specific activities in which I feel in my element are:

* ....

* ....

* ....

2) You can put yourself into more situations in which you are in your element.

This is the crucial part. Great football managers, for example, select players to play in their best position. Why? Because that is where the player has what is called 'personal radar'. They know what is going to happen before it happens. Great managers in business follow a similar rule. They put people in the places where they perform at their best. You will also have a sixth sense in certain situations. Try completing the following sentence.

The things I can do to put myself into more situations where I am in element are:

* ....

* ....

* ....

3) You can keep improving when you are in your element.

Put yourself in those situations and keep improving. How to make this happen? One approach is to maintain good habits. When working with peak performers, for example, I encouraged them to keep something called *My Right Book*. Looking at their daily work, they were asked to record: a) Three things I did right today – and how I can do more of these things in the future: b) Two things I can do better in the future – and how. They then got into the habit of constant improvement. Try completing the following sentence.

Strengths

The things I can do to keep improving when I am in my element are:

* ....

* ....

* ....

"Do what you do best and do it brilliantly," we are told. The key is to keep putting yourself in your element – the place where you do what you enjoy, feel at ease and excel. You are then more likely to achieve peak performance.

3 tips for recognising where you go 'a, b ____ then leap to ____ z'

Peak performers see the destination quickly. The architect walks onto a site and visualises the finished house. The footballer sees the defence-splitting pass that will create a goal. The counsellor greets the troubled child and knows how they want the child to be feeling after their conversation. When entering the situation in which they excel, peak performers quickly see the picture of perfection. They go 'a, b ___ then leap to ___ z'. Let's explore where you have this ability.

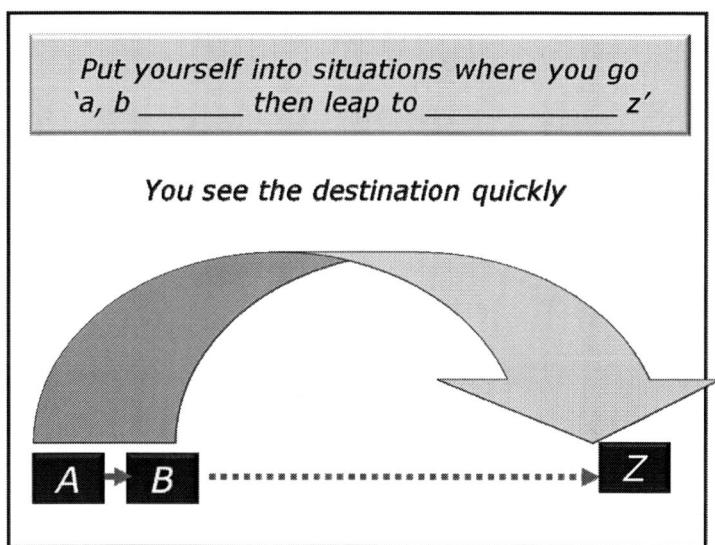

1) You can clarify where you quickly go 'a, b ___ z'.

Everybody has a place where they think strategically and quickly see the solution. The MD of a High Street chain explained: "I love retail. Put me in any shop anywhere in the world and I show how it can

Strengths

make better profits. My wife thinks I am crazy, because on Sundays I want to take her shopping. Every Saturday morning I went shopping with my mother. I remember gazing at the fishmonger's shop and, in my mind's eye, imagining how it could be rearranged. Now I do that for a living." Where does this happen for you? Depending on your natural talent, you may quickly see the destination when fixing a car engine, solving a financial problem, designing a workshop or whatever. Try tackling the exercise on this theme and complete the following sentence.

The specific situation in which I go 'a, b ___ and then leap to ___ z' is:

* ....

2) You can clarify what you do right to actually deliver 'z'.

Peak performers are often intuitive. Asked to explain their technique, they reply: "I just do it." A gifted salesperson, for example, may start by imagining what they want the customer to be saying, thinking and feeling when leaving the shop. For instance: "The salesperson really listened to me. They found out what I wanted and offered several options. Nothing was too much trouble. I got what I wanted and will recommend the shop to friends." The salesperson will approach the customer, quickly try several different strategies and see what works. They will then do whatever is required to ensure the customer is satisfied when they leave the shop. Every achiever has their individual approach to delivering 'z'. Going beyond the "I just do it," explanation, however, many go through the following phases.

- **Preparation**

Because they are fascinated by the subject, they rehearse many potential scenarios. They have what Arie De Geus called 'a memory of the future'. When preparing for a particular assignment, they 'practise until they can forget'. Before entering the 'arena', they relax, re-centre and refocus.

The Strengths Toolbox

- **Professionalism**

Going into the situation, they feel alive and alert. Using their 'antennae', they scan what is happening and look for patterns. Seeing the desired goal, they clarify their strategy. Putting their plan into action, they keep doing the right things in the right way until they reach their goal.

- **Peak performance**

"Sometimes I win games by producing 8/10," said one tennis player. "Other times I must play to my full potential and produce 10/10." Achievers sometimes also add that 'touch of class' and do something special to deliver the goods. How do you reach the goal? Try completing the following sentence.

The specific things I do to actually deliver 'z' are:

* ....
* ....
* ....

3) You can put yourself into more situations where you quickly see 'z'.

Wayne Gretzky, the greatest ice hockey goal scorer in North American history, was once asked: "What is the secret behind why you score so many goals?" His reply was: "A good hockey player plays where the puck is. A great hockey player plays where the puck is going to be." Gretzky aimed: 'to skate to the part of the rink where the puck will appear.' Geniuses have this sixth sense: they know what is going to happen before it happens. Keep putting yourself into situations where this happens for you, because this is where you have natural genius. Try completing the following sentence.

Strengths

The things I can do to put myself into more situations where I quickly see 'z' are

* ....

* ....

* ....

3 tips for employing your personal radar

Peak performers have a sixth sense in the areas where they perform brilliantly. They seem to know 'what will happen before it happens'. Al Siebert, author of *The Survivor Personality*, called this gift 'personal radar'. Let's explore where you might use your radar and repertoire to deliver great results.

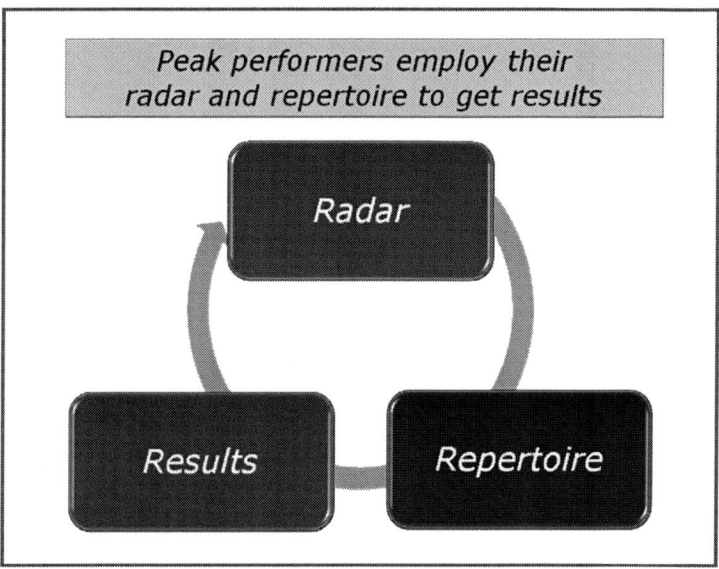

1) You can clarify where you have good radar.

What are the situations in which you have good radar? Where do you quickly see patterns? Where do you quickly see the desired picture of perfection? Different people have different kinds of radar. Great footballers, for example, seem to have more time and space than other players. Demonstrating superb positional sense, they seem several moves ahead of the opposition. Great retailers have an intuitive 'feeling' for their business. They can predict what will be happening in the market in the future. Ellen MacArthur, the round-the-world yachtswoman, reads the waves to anticipate future sailing

Strengths

conditions. Processing the information, she then works out the strategy for reaching her destination.

So what happens when people use their personal radar? Entering the situation in which they excel, they feel alive and alert. Employing their antennae, they rapidly gather information about three things. a) They see patterns and, extrapolating the patterns, they envisage potential scenarios. b) They see the desired picture of perfection. c) They see how to pursue the best strategy for achieving the picture of perfection. You will have good radar in some situations, but not in others. For example, you may work well with certain clients, but not with others. (Be aware of where you have bad radar and develop a strategy for dealing with those situations.) Try completing the following sentence.

The specific situation in which I have good radar is:

* ....

2) You can clarify what you have in your repertoire.

Radar provides lots of information – but it is only the starting point. People must dig into their repertoire to reach their goals. There are normally three components in your repertoire. a) Strengths – the natural talents you have been given. b) Strategies – the life experience, knowledge, models and wisdom you have gathered. c) Skills – the skills, tools and techniques you have developed. Radar is given: but the greatest area of growth lies in expanding your repertoire. Try completing the following sentence.

The strengths, strategies and skills I have in my repertoire that I can use in this situation are:

* ....

* ....

* ....

3) You can use your radar and repertoire to deliver great results.

Faced by a challenging situation, peak performers reach into their repertoire to use the right technique to achieve the desired goal. "Every client is different, but I do follow a certain model," said one counsellor. "Meeting a troubled person, I make them feel welcome and quickly look for behavioural patterns. I then imagine what I want them to be feeling, thinking and saying when they leave the session. Moving on, I try many different strategies to make contact and clarify their goals. Drawing on my experience – yet also staying fully in the present – I then use different tools to help them to succeed." How do you do this in your own way? Try completing the following sentence.

The things I can do to use my radar and repertoire to deliver results in this situation are:

* ....

* ....

* ....

Consider how you can keep putting yourself into situations where you have good radar. You will then increase your chances of doing outstanding work.

3 tips for following your successful style

People develop, they seldom change. This is especially so when pursuing their preferred working style. Everybody has strengths – which is 'What' they do best. Everybody also has a successful style – which is 'How' they work best. Combining these together provides a powerful combination. If you wish, try tackling the exercise on this theme called *My successful style*. This invites you to take the following steps.

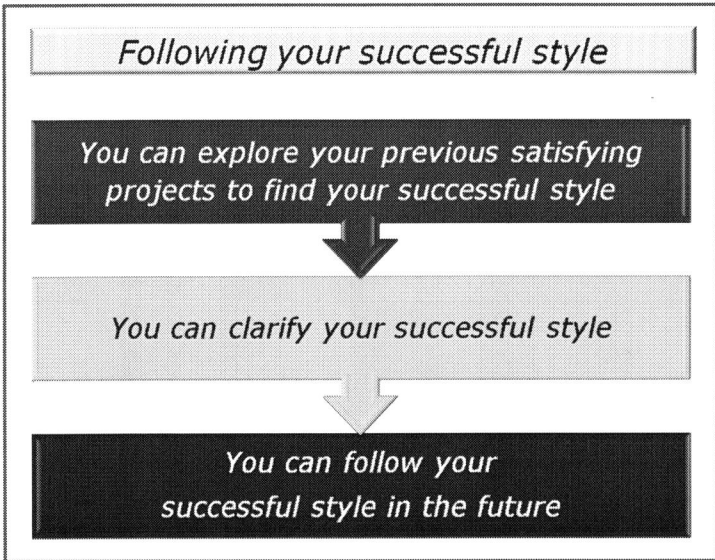

1) You can explore your previous satisfying 'projects' to find your successful style.

Looking back on your life, describe what for you have been 3 stimulating and satisfying projects. Use the term 'project' in the broadest sense. You may have got great satisfaction, for example, from refurbishing a house, designing a web site, launching a product, leading a team, mentoring a particular person, running a workshop or

The Strengths Toolbox

whatever. Exploring each project in turn, describe the specific things that made each one fulfilling.

The first satisfying project was:

* ....

The specific things that made it satisfying were:

* ....

* ....

* ....

The second satisfying project was:

* ....

The specific things that made it satisfying were:

* ....

* ....

* ....

The third satisfying project was:

* ....

The specific things that made it satisfying were:

* ....

* ....

* ....

Strengths

2) You can clarify your successful style.

Looking at each of the projects, can you see any patterns? One person said:

"My pattern is clear – I love building 'prototypes', but several characteristics stand out. First, I must believe the project will improve people's lives. Second, I want to have input into clarifying the 'What' – the goal we want to achieve. Third, I like to have lots of autonomy. Fourth, I prefer to be aiming for a specific deadline. Finally, I love to see the prototype having a positive impact on people's lives."

Looking back on your life, can you see any recurring themes in your satisfying projects? Bearing these in mind, describe what you believe to be your successful style. (You may, of course, have two styles. One where you are working with other people, one when you are working alone.) Try completing the following sentence.

My successful style is that I work best when:

* ....
* ....
* ....

3) You can follow your successful style in the future.

Peak performers follow their preferred working style, which seems to get more pronounced as they get older. The person mentioned above said:

"I want to keep building prototypes, but such jobs are seldom advertised. They are filled ahead of time by people who know what is happening. So that means I must aim to do three things: a) To reach out to potential sponsors in my network: b) To identify their challenges: c) To show how the prototype will help them to succeed. I need to stay ahead of the game, find a potential niche and get backing to build a prototype."

The Strengths Toolbox

Everybody has a preferred way of working, so it is important to find and follow yours. Try completing the final part of the exercise. This can be the key to shaping a fulfilling future.

The steps I can take to follow my successful style in the future are:

* ....

* ....

* ....

3 tips for clarifying your perfect role

We are all self-employed now. There are no jobs anymore – there are only projects. So how can you find or create your perfect niche – and get paid a salary? One approach is to start by clarifying the characteristics of the project, people and place you find stimulating. You can then explore how to get an employer to pay you for delivering these results. After all, people will only hire you if you help them to be successful. Let's consider these steps towards finding your perfect role.

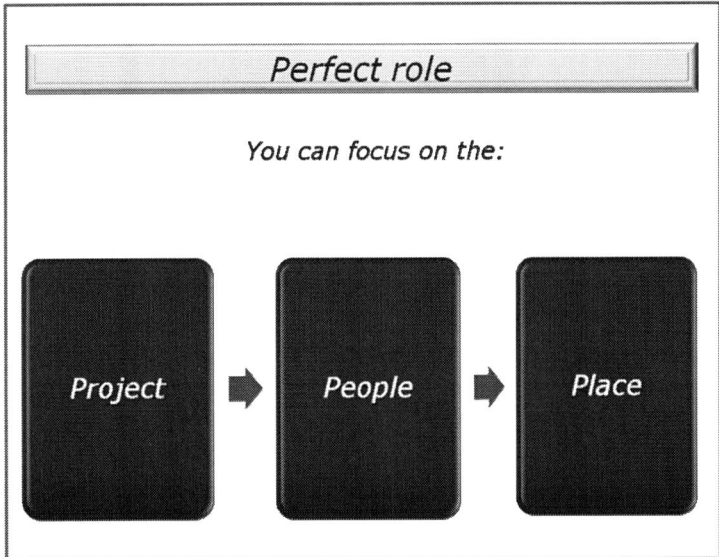

1) Project.

Describe the characteristics of the kind of 'project' you find stimulating. (The 'stimulation factor' must be at least 8/10.) You may enjoy doing 'turnarounds', fixing 'impossible problems', helping people to take charge of their lives, encouraging people to fulfil their potential, leading superb teams, selling ideas or whatever. One person said:

"Looking back on my satisfying 'projects', I can identify several patterns. For example, I love doing work that contributes to improving the quality of people's lives. At university I organised the first ever sponsored 'Fun Run', raising £10k for charity. Early in my IT career I launched software that enabled students to take charge of their own learning. The projects I enjoy normally have a deadline. This forces me to get my act together and make sure that I deliver on time."

What do you find fulfilling? Try completing the following sentence.

The characteristics of the kind of 'project' I find stimulating is one where:

* ....
* ....
* ....

2) People.

Describe the characteristics of the people – both customers and colleagues – that you find stimulating. The person mentioned above said:

"If I am working for a company, I must have a boss I respect. It's best if we agree on the 'What' – the goals to achieve – but I have lots of freedom regarding the 'How'. When leading a team, I must have positive team members who are prepared to work hard. The customers I like are those who are at the forefront of their field. They may be demanding, but they can also make quick decisions."

What people do you work best with? Try completing the following sentence.

The kind of people I find stimulating are:

* ....
* ....
* ....

Strengths

3) Place.

Describe the characteristics of the place – culture and environment – you find stimulating. The person said: "I like working in the 'newer' industries, such as IT and communications. They are professional, informal and are making the rules for the future." So where do you enjoy working? Try completing the following sentence.

The kind of 'place' – culture & environment – I find stimulating is one which is:

* ....
* ....
* ....

Move onto making your action plan. Bearing in mind the answers you have given, describe three things: a) The perfect project: b) The specific results you could deliver to a potential sponsor by delivering this project: c) The steps you can take to find or create such a project. Once you have found it, deliver great work. Try completing the following sentences.

Bearing these answers in mind, my perfect 'project' would be:

* ....

The specific results I could deliver to an employer by doing this project would be:

* ....
* ....
* ....

The Strengths Toolbox

The steps I can take to find or create such a project are:

* ....
* ....
* ....

3 tips for understanding your 'solid ground' and 'dangerous ground'

"I am great working on my solid ground – being with the people with whom I have a values fit," said one person. "This makes up 90% of my job. But sometimes the role takes me into other territory – meeting people with whom there is a mismatch. My style probably upsets them because I speak and think differently. I don't even look right! Sometimes they say things that are like a red flag. Feeling provoked, I speak out of turn. Although I only spend 10% of my time there, it is the dangerous ground where I make mistakes."

Where for you is the solid ground? Where is the dangerous ground? Let's explore how to deal with these different situations.

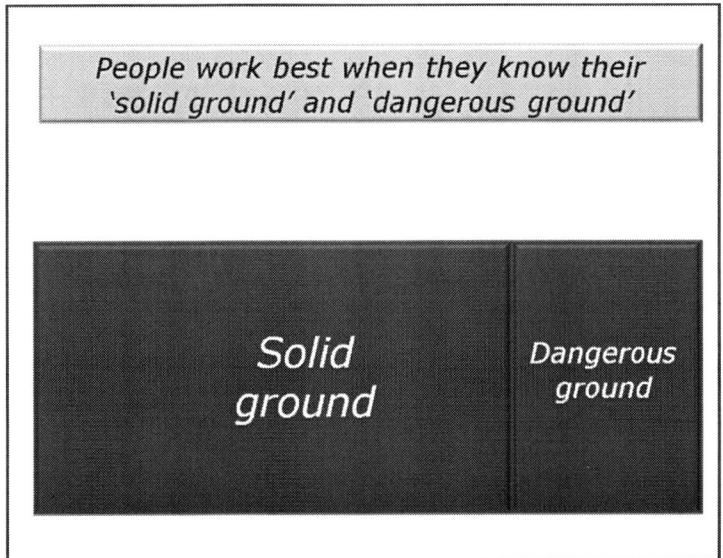

1) You can clarify your 'solid ground'.

Try tackling the exercise on this theme. Describe what for you is the solid ground. You feel comfortable in these situations – but also stretch yourself and do good work. You may be confident because three factors are in place: a) You know your subject; b) You know your audience and their agenda; c) You know how to succeed. Try completing the following sentence.

The situations where I feel on solid ground are:

* ....
* ....
* ....

2) You can clarify your 'dangerous ground'.

Describe what for you is dangerous ground. These may be situations where either: a) Your values don't fit; b) Your communication style is too different; c) You do not respect the people and this occasionally slips through; d) You feel so passionately about a subject that you may become aggressive or opinionated; e) You commit a cultural 'sin' – and sometimes you don't even know you have done it! Try completing the following sentence.

The situations where I feel on dangerous ground are:

* ....
* ....
* ....

3) You can build on the solid ground and deal with the dangerous ground.

Let's start by focusing on the solid ground. How can you continue to build on your strengths? How can you put yourself into more situations where you work best? How can you reach more people with whom you have a values fit? How can you help them to

Strengths

succeed? How can you keep expanding the solid ground?

Let's examine where you must tread carefully. How can you avoid putting yourself in these places? If you must do so, how can you prepare properly? How can you discover people's agendas? How can you rehearse? What might be the red flags? How can you manage potentially difficult moments? How can you keep your concentration? How can you be super professional?

Peak performers tend to stay on solid ground. They do what they do best in the places where they perform best. Frequently this happens after years spent trying to reach different audiences – but then they decide to focus. Committed to constant improvement, they continually use their imagination to innovate. But they do this in places where their contribution – their art or work – is appreciated. Trying to change their offering to reach a different audience can become their own dangerous ground. It is important to connect with people, but not at the expense of diluting their 'A' talent.

Conclude the exercise by describing two things: a) How you can build on the solid ground; b) How you can deal with the dangerous ground. Do your best in every situation – but focus on the projects, people and places where you can use your strengths. Try completing the following sentences.

The things I can do to build on the solid ground are:

* ....

* ....

* ....

The things I can do to deal with the dangerous ground are:

* ....

* ....

* ....

3 tips for clarifying your perfect customer

Imagine you are a freelancer. Whilst you continue to deliver great service to your present customers, some of your week is spent searching for new work. Whilst it may seem unrealistic to be choosy – especially if you don't yet have any customers – it is useful to clarify your perfect target group. (If you are a full-time employee in an organisation, the equivalent of this approach is to identify and work for your perfect manager.)

We work best with kindred spirits – people who share similar professional values. We can then start off at 7/10, which provides a springboard for getting to 10/10. You will, of course, continue to do a professional job with all clients. The key to building a long-term business, however, is to work with your perfect customers. Here are three ideas for identifying this target group.

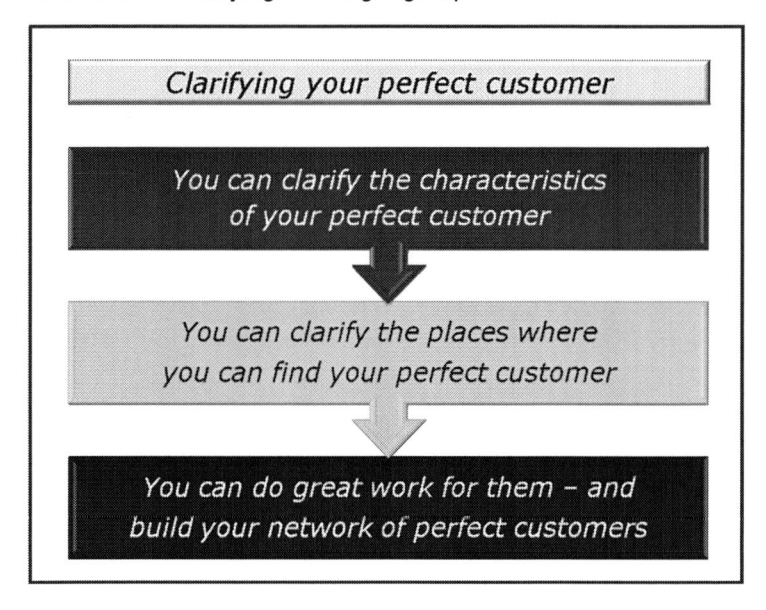

Clarifying your perfect customer

You can clarify the characteristics of your perfect customer

⬇

You can clarify the places where you can find your perfect customer

⬇

You can do great work for them – and build your network of perfect customers

1) You can clarify the characteristics of your perfect customer.

How to make this happen? Start by identifying the customers with whom you work best. Who are your favourite customers? Which give you positive energy? What are the personality characteristics of these customers? What are their values? One person said:

"I work best with people who are positive achievers. They love to set goals, work hard and achieve success. I guess many people would describe similar characteristics, but I have deliberately targeted these kinds of customers. Many of my clients have 'humanistic' values. They want to create an inspiring environment that encourages people to do their best. At the same time, however, they are prepared to take tough decisions."

Try tackling the exercise on this theme called *My perfect customer*. Begin by completing the following sentences.

My perfect customer

*The characteristics of
my perfect customer are:*

* _____

* _____

* _____

* _____

2) *You can clarify the places where you can find your perfect customer.*

"I like working with customers who are 'making the new rules' of work," said one freelancer. "So most of my clients are in high tech or new media. I am not good at working with people in finance or banking who want to improve the efficiency of existing systems. This has implications – because many start-ups are rather cash strapped. So I need to keep staying in touch with many potential clients, rather than rely on two or three who might provide long-term contracts."

Looking at the characteristics of your perfect customers, where are you likely to find such people? Do you work best with people in certain roles, such as decision makers, managers, knowledge workers, front-liners or other people? Do you prefer working with people in the public or private sector – in high tech, retail, leisure or finance? Try completing the following sentence.

The places where I am more likely to find my perfect customer are:

* ....
* ....
* ....

3) *You can do great work for them – and build your network of perfect customers.*

Do great work that helps them to achieve success. Personal recommendation is always the best advert – and it is likely that they will know others who share similar characteristics. Provide them with great service and they may recommend you to other people. This isn't guaranteed, but it is the likeliest way of building a good customer network – and more than 80% of future work will come from your network. Try completing the following sentence.

Strengths

The specific things I can do to perform great work for my perfect customer are:

* ....

* ....

* ....

3 tips for reaching out to potential sponsors

How can you make a living doing what you love – inside or outside an organisation? There are several rules for finding sponsors. These apply whether you are a freelancer or seeking fresh challenges within an organisation. As we know, people often buy from those they already know in their network. So potential 'sellers' are told to go out and 'network'. But real networking is not about self-promotion. It is about helping others to succeed. If you help others to succeed, however, you are more likely to get hired by sponsors. Let's explore how this works in practice.

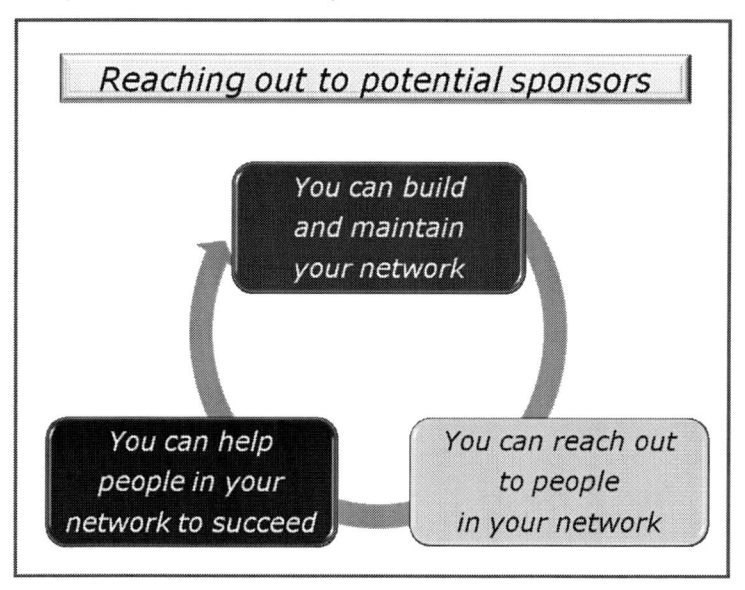

Reaching out to potential sponsors

- You can build and maintain your network
- You can reach out to people in your network
- You can help people in your network to succeed

1) You can build and maintain your network.

How to find work? There is both good news and bad news. The bad news is that old-style methods of job search resemble a lottery and destroy confidence. The good news is that 'people buy people'. Why? In an increasingly unpredictable world, leaders want to buy 'predictability'. So they prefer to hire somebody they know who has a good track record. They can then build on the person's strengths and find ways to compensate for their weaknesses.

"More than 90% of my work comes from my network," said one freelancer. "The hard part is getting started. You must spend masses of time visiting people, sharing know-how and helping them to succeed. Providing you keep planting seeds, sooner or later somebody will say: 'How can we take this further?' You make clear contracts, do superb work and deliver success. Then you just keep networking."

Start by drawing a map of your network. (See below.) If you are an employee and want to stay in your organisation, write the names of people you know, those you admire and those with whom you can think of working. If you are a freelancer, write the names of every potential sponsor in every organisation.

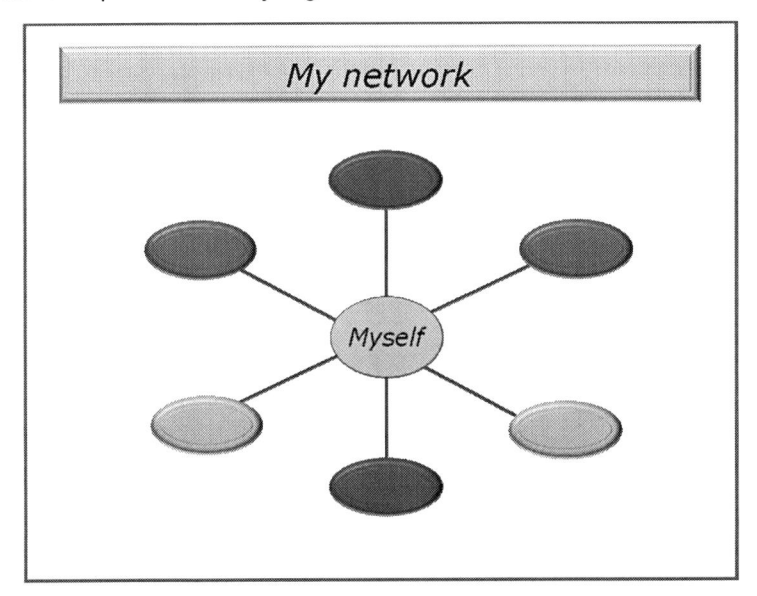

My network

Myself

2) *You can reach out to people in your network.*

How to make this happen? Some people suggest the route of cold calling or direct mail, but it is important to be a giver, rather than a taker. It is vital:

a) To reach out to people in a way that fits your values system.

b) To recognise that real networking is about helping other people to succeed – it is not about self-promotion.

c) To meet people face-to-face, explore the challenges they face and share knowledge that will help them to succeed.

Follow your natural way of networking. Do things that put a spring in your step. As a writer, for example, it is natural for me to send people free copies of the latest exercise, article or book. The key is to find your way. You might want to recommend books, gift a session on a client's 'away day' or connect people by putting them in touch with each other.

Do something every day to reach some people in your network. Keep planting seeds – but be patient. It may take up to a year investing time in potential sponsors before the right opportunity appears. Remember: people buy face-to-face, so find a way to visit them. Most of your future work will come from present customers – so increase the chances of meeting. For example, if you have a 2.00 pm appointment with a current customer, arrive at 12.00. Sit in their Atrium or restaurant and do e-mails. You will find that individuals will pass by and say: "I was thinking about you the other day. Could you help us with.....?"

3) *You can help people in your network to succeed.*

Let's return to the key point. Real networking is about helping other people to succeed. It is always about the other person, it is never about you. So when meeting potential sponsors, after a short while ask them: "What are the key challenges you face? What is your picture of success? What are the real results you want to achieve?" Share knowledge, ideas and tools that will help them to achieve their goals. If appropriate, sit alongside them and do some creative problem solving. Try completing the following sentence.

Strengths

The specific things I can do to help the people in my network to succeed are:

* ....

* ....

* ....

Keep giving to people. Providing you plant enough seeds, eventually somebody will say: "How can we take this further?" You can then move onto the next stage – making clear contracts about how you can work together.

3 tips for making clear contracts with sponsors

Contracting is crucial in any relationship. This is especially so when providing a service to a customer or agreeing goals with your manager. Let's focus on three steps for making clear contracts with sponsors.

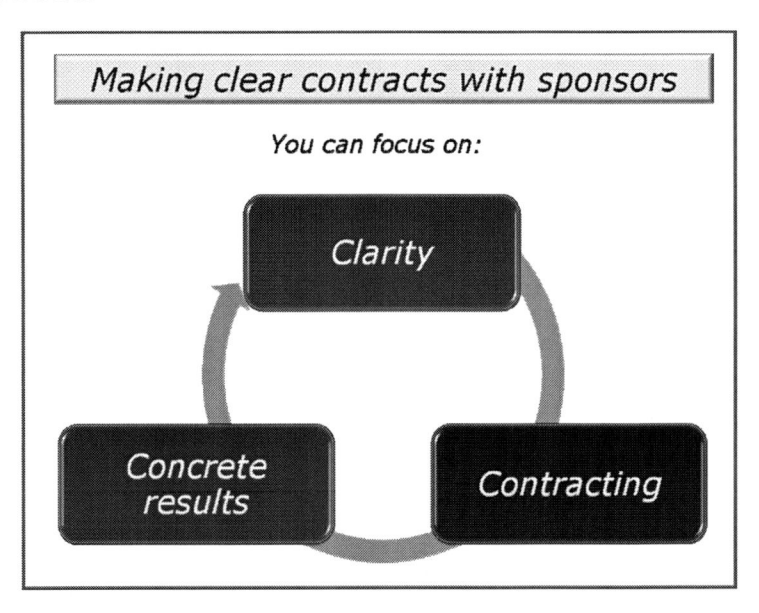

Making clear contracts with sponsors

You can focus on:

- Clarity
- Contracting
- Concrete results

1) You can focus on clarity.

Start by making crystal clear contracts about the 'What'. If appropriate, ask the sponsor: "What are the real results you want to achieve? What is your picture of perfection? What will be happening that will show we have achieved success?" Clarify what must be delivered and by when. Play back your understanding to make sure you both have the same picture.

"Sounds okay, but what if my sponsor doesn't have a clear picture or has not yet formulated their goals?" somebody may ask. If this is the case, be proactive and super professional. Decision makers want to improve one or more of the 3 Ps: their profits, their product quality – service quality – and their people. Looking at the world from their point of view, consider the challenges they face. Clarify what you believe may be their picture of success. Bearing these goals in mind, clarify what you can deliver to help them achieve these results. Translate these into deliverables and share these targets with your sponsor. You can then clarify the agreed picture. If the sponsor is still unclear, consider finding another boss. Clarity is crucial if you are going to have any chance of success.

Imagine you are aiming to work with a sponsor. They may be an external client, your manager or a new boss inside your organisation. Try completing the following sentence.

Clarity. The things I can do to establish clarity about the real results they want to achieve are:

* ....
* ....
* ....

2) You can focus on contracting.

Agree the 'What' – then move to the 'How'. Clarify the broad principles of 'how' the sponsor would like you to work to reach the goals. (A warning sign can be bosses who lay out a 'painting by numbers' process that they will aim to police.) Clarify the Dos and Don'ts for working well with the sponsor. Say how you will proactively keep them informed. Agree on the resources needed to deliver the picture of perfection. For example, make sure you have the right balance of accountability, autonomy and authority.

"Certainly I am prepared to be held accountable," said one manager, "but I also require autonomy and authority. My last job turned into a disaster. Flattered to be approached, I accepted the role without making clear contracts. Accountable for turning around a team and hitting a huge financial target, I did not clarify the autonomy

The Strengths Toolbox

and authority. When aiming to make radical changes in the team, for example, the company said I must keep the same people. So I was trying to climb a mountain with several people who did not want to be mountaineers. Now I make crystal clear contracts before taking a new role."

Conclude the contracting session by, yet again, 'playing back' what you believe to be the 'What', 'How' and 'When'. If appropriate, put it in writing, such as an email or project plan. Certainly it is okay for contracts to evolve – that is a fact of life. The re-contracting proves can then be done by referring to the original agreement, clarifying what has changed and working together towards the new agreed picture.

Let's return to the sponsor with whom you want to make clear contracts. Try completing the following sentence.

Contracting. The things I can do to make clear contracts about the Dos & Don'ts for working with them are:

* ....

* ....

* ....

3) *You can focus on concrete results.*

Sponsors need reassurance – so produce some quick results. That will buy time and give you chance to get on with the work. If you are leading a team, for example, gather people together and ask yourselves:

"How can we produce some early successes? How can we be proactive and keep our sponsors informed? If we were outside suppliers on a 6 month rolling contract, how would we behave? Would we behave any differently from what we do now? How can we display the same sense of urgency, stay close to our sponsors and help them to succeed? When are the key dates – such as the quarterly reviews, etc – when the sponsors will make emotional decisions about whether or not we are delivering the goods? How

Strengths

can we stay ahead of the game, anticipate their agendas and keep satisfying our sponsors? How can we build a reputation for delivery?"

Let's return to the sponsor for whom you want to deliver success. Try completing the following sentence.

Concrete results. The things I can do to deliver concrete results for them are:

* ....

* ....

* ....

Great performers follow this discipline all the time. They continue to keep in touch with their sponsors and focus on clarity, contracting and concrete results. This provides the platform for achieving ongoing success.

3 tips for managing sponsors by focusing on the '3 Rs'

Peter Drucker once wrote: "The purpose of business is to create and keep a customer." The same rule applies when each of us contribute to an organisation. Whether we work as a freelancer or as a full-time employee, our role is to satisfy our sponsors – the people who can hire or fire us. Some people forget this rule and become institutionalised. They stop taking initiatives and wait to be 'managed'. Many of today's businesses, however, want people who are positive, proactive and professional. Let's explore how you can manage your sponsors. This calls for taking responsibility, reassuring them and delivering results.

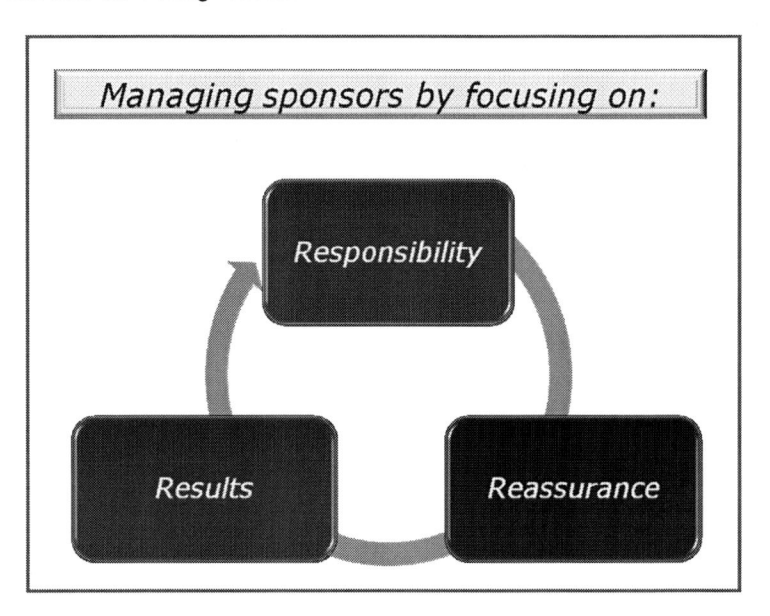

Managing sponsors by focusing on:

- Responsibility
- Reassurance
- Results

1) You can take responsibility.

"I want people to step forward," said one leader. "I want them: a) To understand our goals: b) To say how they want to contribute: c) To

Strengths

deliver on their promises. Too many people sit waiting for me to dish out the jobs. That may have worked in the past, but now I want self-managing people who take initiatives. This frees me up to take a more strategic role in shaping the business."

Writing in the 1980s, Peter Drucker predicted the need for people to behave like 'volunteers' in organisations. This calls for three things. a) For the leaders to provide a compelling vision; b) For the individuals to 'opt-in' and behave likes volunteers, rather than victims; c) For the organisation to provide the support that people need to achieve the vision. This may or may not happen in your organisation, but taking initiatives plays a crucial part in satisfying your sponsor. Try completing the following sentence.

The specific things I can do to take responsibility are:

* ....
* ....
* ....

2) You can reassure your sponsors.

Sponsors worry. They go to bed at night worrying about hitting the numbers, satisfying their bosses, improving service quality, getting the right people and staying out of trouble. Similarly, their bosses are under pressure from the banks, stock market or other outside forces. Your job is to reassure them. Never say: "Trust me." That is like a red flag to a bull.

Show sponsors that you understand the business. Make clear contracts about your contribution, keep them informed and deliver early successes. Sponsors do not like nasty surprises. So manage their expectations. Be honest, especially when faced by potential crises. Show you have considered the possible ways forward, the respective consequences and, where appropriate, give your recommendations. Try completing the following sentence.

The Strengths Toolbox

The specific things I can do to reassure my sponsors are:

* ....

* ....

* ....

3) *You can deliver results.*

"Football is a results business," said one leading manager. "I can talk a good game with the press, but I must deliver results on the field. Otherwise I will get sacked."

Sponsors will judge you by your results. This calls for doing three things. First, being crystal clear on what you must deliver. Second, doing superb work and delivering the goods. Third, going that extra mile and producing something special. The final point is vital. People buy people and, in the future, they will remember if you gave them great service. Taking these steps will enable you to create and keep customers. Try completing the following sentences.

The specific things I can do to deliver results to my sponsors are:

* ....

* ....

* ....

3 tips for being of 'high value & hard to replace'

The world of work is constantly changing – so how can you continue to make yourself employable? "Build on your strengths, find sponsors who will pay you and deliver success," is the mantra. Sounds okay – but how can you stay ahead of the game? Here are three tips for maintaining your employability.

1) You can recognise where you are on the employability scale.

Take a look at *The Employability Model*. This plots your 'Value' to an employer against your 'Replaceability'. (Nobody is irreplaceable, but some are more replaceable than others.)

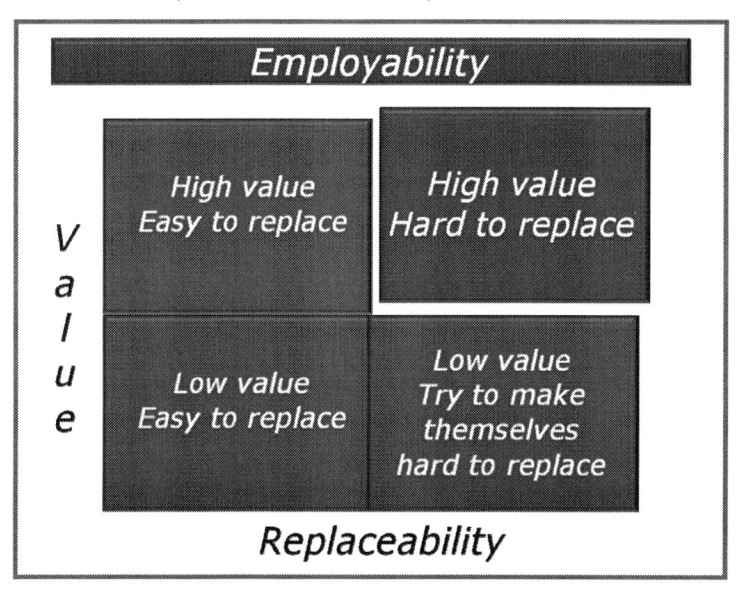

	Employability	
V **a** **l** **u** **e**	High value Easy to replace	High value Hard to replace
	Low value Easy to replace	Low value Try to make themselves hard to replace
	Replaceability	

Looking through the eyes of a potential employer, where do you fit on the model? Is your contribution:

- **High value/Easy to replace**

For example, some older-style marketing departments fall into this category. Some marketers are great – because they align their efforts to the business strategy. Some do their own thing – whether or not this supports the business. Those who fall into the latter category may well become candidates for outsourcing.

- **Low value/Easy to replace**

For example, cleaners and consultants. "When in doubt, keep the cleaners," we are told. "They are cheaper and get more visible results." Joking aside, it is vital for people to move out of this quadrant, otherwise they become cannon fodder.

- **Low value/Try to make themselves hard to replace**

For example, departments that attempt to make themselves hard to replace by obscuring their work in the 'black arts'. IT, Business Intelligence and Finance may soon be on this danger list.

- **High value/Hard to replace**

For example, brilliant niche providers who perform outstanding work, but are also willing to pass on their wisdom. Paradoxically, they make themselves valuable by giving away their knowledge, rather than by hoarding trade secrets.

2) *You can make yourself of 'high value & hard to replace'.*

Try tackling the exercise at the end of this piece called *Employability*. Start by describing where you rate yourself now on the scale of value and replaceability. Then move onto the next stage. Describe the specific things you can do to make yourself of 'high value & hard to replace'. Here is how one person tackled the challenge.

"Ten years ago I was one of the few people running creativity workshops in this country," they explained. "Five years ago the market suddenly became flooded with people offering courses in this field. What to do? Certainly it was a test of my creativity!"

Strengths

"Going back to basics, I visited at least four customers every week, but this time focused on 'applied creativity'. When setting up the visit, I offered to meet any person or team interested in using creative techniques to tackle specific business challenges. The sessions were fun and produced many practical solutions. Since then I have run literally hundreds of sessions in 'applied creativity'. People are happy to pay because the approach delivers tangible business results."

3) You can continue to make yourself employable in the future.

How can you stay in the top right corner? Some of the eternal rules apply: a) Stay close to your customers; b) Encourage them talk about their present and future challenges; c) Do whatever you can to help them tackle the challenges and achieve success.

Spend a lot of time with your 'pacesetting' customers. Pacesetters take the lead, maintain the lead and extend the lead. They make the new rules for the game. Staying close to such customers provides an advantage. They are tackling challenges today that others will tackle tomorrow. Working with pacesetters helps you to stay ahead of the game. You will then be in a better position to provide services that are of high value & hard to replace. Try tackling the exercise below to make sure you continue to be employable in the future.

Employability

The place I rate myself now on the scale of value and replaceability is:

* ....

The things I can do to make myself of high value & hard to replace are:

* ....

* ....

* ....

The Strengths Toolbox

The things I can do to continue to make myself of high value & hard to replace in the future are:

* ....

* ....

* ....

3 tips for balancing the great work and grunt work

How can you balance your great work and grunt work? People do not mind doing tough jobs – even boring tasks – providing they can see the point. But they don't like doing grunt work that doesn't make sense. The frequently quoted 'cathedral story' still holds true. Ask one labourer what he is doing and he answers: "I am mixing cement." Ask another labourer doing exactly the same job and he says: "I am building a cathedral." Guess who is happier. Let's explore three steps towards doing fine work.

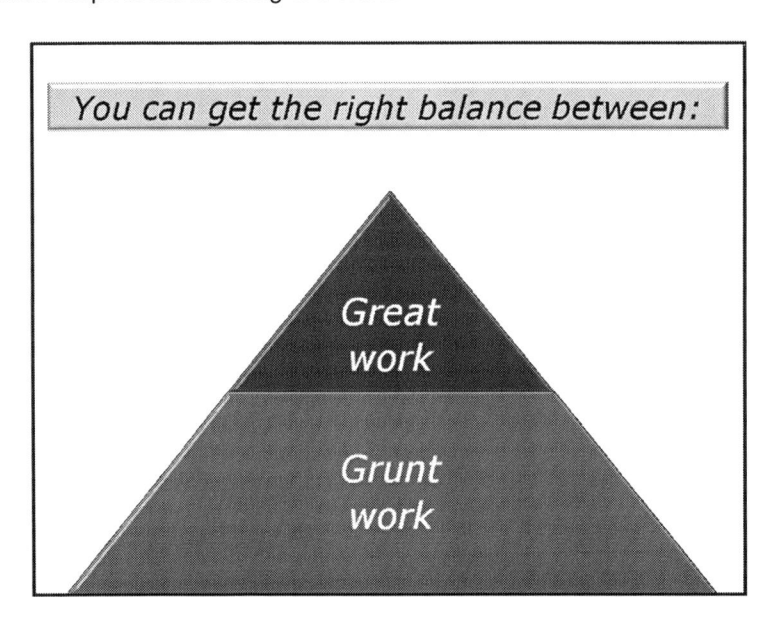

You can get the right balance between:

Great work

Grunt work

1) You can choose to do a specific piece of great work.

Sometimes this part is relatively easy – you may have lots of projects and dreams. Sometimes it is more difficult – you may have to find or

The Strengths Toolbox

create a space in the jungle. One manager took the second route – and finally ended up doing the job he was hired to perform. He explained:

"Two years ago I took several steps that rejuvenated my career. Looking at my diary for the next six months, I couldn't see where I would get my creative kicks. Supposedly I had been hired to lead a pioneering team – but my days were spent managing, rather than leading.

"Then I got savvy. I decided: a) To deliver the goals I had been set in my day job; b) To, on top of this, do something special that benefited the business. Looking ahead, I decided to manage my day job, but also do a great piece of work with customers. Six months later we presented the improved customer satisfaction scores at the company conference.

"'This is exactly what we hired you to do,' said my bosses. Meeting them 2 weeks later, I outlined three specific projects we could do to benefit the bottom line, but it meant re-focusing our resources. Seeing the sense in the argument, they gave the go-ahead. Now we concentrate on doing a few pioneering projects."

Try tackling the exercise on this theme called *Great work & grunt work*. Start by describing a specific piece of great work you would like to complete—then move onto the next stage.

Great work. The specific piece of great work I would like to complete is:

* ....

2) *You can do the necessary grunt work.*

Now comes the interesting part. Peak performers dream, do and deliver – which means following certain daily disciplines. Imagine you are an athlete aiming to compete in the Olympic final. Starting from this destination and working backwards, you will make a clear project plan – mapping out what must be done each year, each month and each day. You will get started by launching into following a daily rhythm. The same is true for any project. There may be grunt work involved – but it makes sense on the road to achieving the great

Strengths

work. Encouraging yourself on the journey, you will keep working hard to ensure you reach the final stage.

Grunt work. The steps I can take to plan and do the necessary grunt work are:

* ....
* ....
* ....

3) *You can finally produce the piece of great work.*

Sometimes you will make a superhuman effort to finish – sometimes you will simply flow, focus and finish. Good finishers keep their eyes on the goal but, paradoxically, also pay as much attention to the process as the prize. Staying concentrated in the moment, they may find the fruit drops into their hands. Aiming to perform outstanding work, you will also frequently add that 'touch of class'. How can you do this in your way? How can you become a 'class act'? Great design is simple, beautiful and effective. You may well follow similar rules and when producing something worthwhile – something that benefits people. The grunt work will then make sense on the road to producing great work. Try completing the final part of the exercise.

Great work. The steps I can then take to produce the piece of great work are:

* ....
* ....
* ....

3 tips for practising the art of mental rehearsal

Peak performers relax and rehearse to get great results. "My best performances come after preparing properly," said one person. "The times when I have messed up – and failed to deliver the right results – have been when I didn't relax or rehearse properly." Here are three steps you can focus on for practising the art of mental rehearsal.

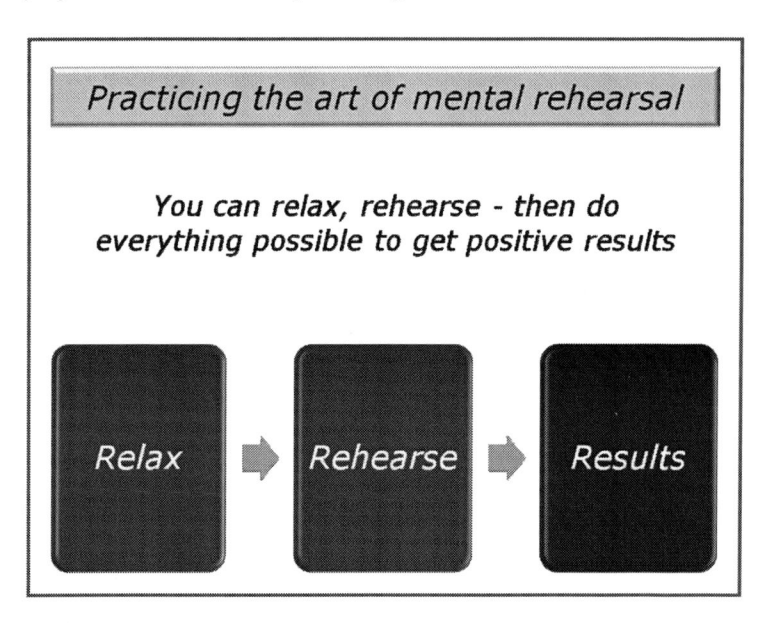

Practicing the art of mental rehearsal

You can relax, rehearse - then do everything possible to get positive results

Relax ➡ **Rehearse** ➡ **Results**

1) You can relax.

Start by looking ahead to a challenging situation. You may want to perform at your best when giving a presentation, playing a football match, solving a conflict or whatever. Starting from your destination – the date when you will enter the arena – build in time to conserve your energy ahead of time. Get enough sleep, otherwise you may feel edgy. Different people relax in different ways. Some set aside quiet time to plan; some lie in the bath rehearsing the day ahead; some arrive an hour before a customer appointment to sit in the car park gathering their thoughts. What is your method? Try completing the following sentences.

Looking into the future, the challenging situation where I want to perform at my best is:

* ....

The specific things I can do to make sure I rest and relax properly before entering the situation are:

* ....

* ....

* ....

2) *You can rehearse.*

Relax, re-focus and rehearse. Looking ahead to the situation, ask yourself:

- What are the *real results* I want to achieve? What is my picture of perfection? What are the actual words I want people to be saying after the session?

- How can I do my best achieve this result? What are the three key things I can do to give myself the greatest chance of success? How can I put these things into practice?

- What are the many possible scenarios? What is the best that can happen – and how can I build on this success? What is the worst that can happen? How can I prevent this happening? How can do my best if it does happen? What are the difficult questions people may ask? How can I answer these questions in a good way?

Settle on your chosen strategy – then practise what must be done to

The Strengths Toolbox

achieve the goals. Keep practising and 'practise until you can forget.' Try completing the following sentence – then relax before the next stage.

The specific things I can do to make sure I rehearse properly before entering the situation are:

* ....
* ....
* ....

3) *You can do your best to get the positive results.*

Relax and re-centre. Refocus on the results you want to achieve – the picture of perfection. Peak performers often have an individual ritual they use to snap into 'alert mode' before entering the arena – be it going onto the football field, making a customer presentation or whatever. You will have your own ritual. Be fully present. You can then give your full attention to the situation, person or challenge. Take a final moment to gather your thoughts. Go into the arena and follow your chosen strategy. Be fully alert and use your antennae to be aware of what is happening. Take these things into account and, if necessary, be prepared to change tack – but also keep your eyes on the goal. If you hit a setback, buy time to re-gather your thoughts, then pursue your chosen way forward. Keep giving 100%. Do everything possible to deliver the results. Flow, focus and finish. Try completing the following sentence.

The specific things I can do to do my best to get positive results in the situation are:

* ....
* ....
* ....

3 tips for being able to flow – rather than freeze

Think of a situation in which you want to flow, rather than freeze. You may be giving a keynote speech, singing in a musical, playing in a cup final or whatever. Here are three things you can do to be at your best – rather than be consumed by fear, flee or become frustrated. Fighting spirit may well be needed. But it is important to fight fair, rather than dirty. This will provide the springboard for you to flow and succeed.

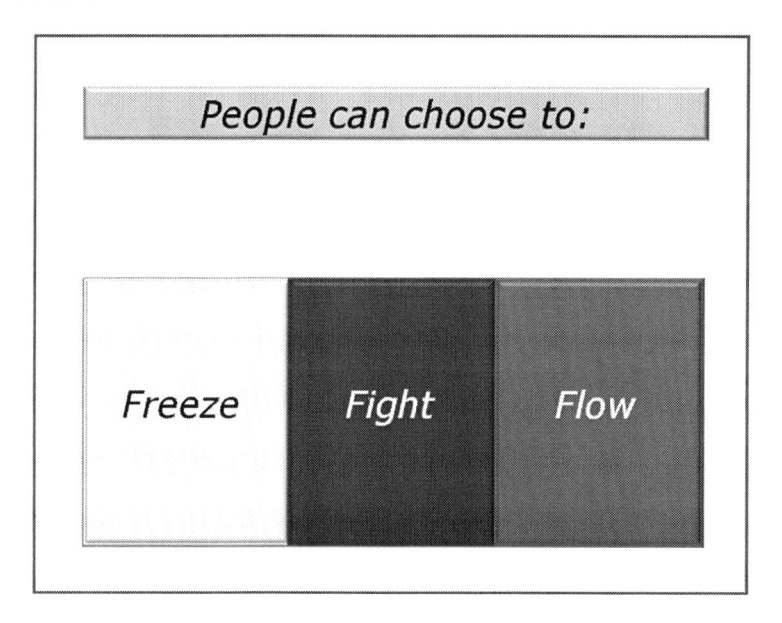

People can choose to:

| Freeze | Fight | Flow |

1) You can rehearse the situation in which you want to flow.

"Ever since I was 6 years old, I had imagined sinking the final putt to win a major championship," said the professional golfer. "Now the moment had arrived. People said the crowd became hushed, but I never noticed. Going inside my 'bubble', I went through the old routine. This was just me, the ball, the green and the hole. Breathing calmly, I remembered the putts I had holed – rather than those I had missed – and concentrated on the moment. Swinging the putter, I made perfect contact – and watched the ball travel into the hole. All hell broke loose and I collapsed in a heap."

How can you rehearse properly? Picture the situation in which you want to flow – then go through the following steps.

a) Start from the destination – the end goal.

Clarify the picture of perfection. Describe what you want people to be saying, feeling and thinking after you have finished. Focus on the real results you want to achieve.

b) Return to the beginning – the time before you enter the 'arena' – and map out the total journey.

Describe how you will prepare. List every step in detail. Move onto the day of the 'performance'. Consider how you will get yourself into the right frame of mind. How will you enter the arena? Describe how you will behave in the first minute, ten minutes and so on. Continue until you have completed the performance.

c) Clarify how you will 'flow' when you are 'on stage'.

Looking back on your life, recall times when you have done your best in similar situations. What did you do right then? Looking ahead, how can you follow similar principles during the 'performance'? Once you are happy with your plans, throw in some curve balls. Consider the potential difficult scenarios and, exploring each one in turn, clarify how you will get back on course. Continue until everything is covered. Then relax and look forward to the performance.

2) You can go into the situation and flow.

In the film *Billy Elliott*, the hero is asked what he feels like when dancing. Billy finds it hard to reply at first, but then he says it is as if he 'disappears'. "Like I feel a change in my whole body...And I've got this fire in my body....Like electricity." Maybe he was describing 'going into the zone' – maybe about being able to flow. How can you do that in your chosen field?

Be fully present. Relax, re-centre and focus on the desired results. Be alert and use your antennae to be aware of what is happening. Do what ever it takes to get to 8/10. Then add that touch of class to achieve the 10/10. Flow, focus, finish and, maybe as a by-product, find fulfilment.

3) You can re-centre after setbacks and recover your flow.

Great performers continually rehearse potential scenarios in their chosen field. When these events happen, they are several steps ahead of other people. Looking ahead to your 'performance', you will have rehearsed: a) The things that can go wrong – and how you will manage these difficulties; b) The things that can go right – and how you can build on these successes.

"Spontaneity takes a lot of planning," we are told. You have anticipated the potential scenarios, so will have many solutions in your kit bag. What is something unexpected happens? Certainly you may quickly go through the stages of the 'reactive change curve': shock, denial, paralysis, anger, hurt, healing, new strength, new goals, hard work—then eventually success and self-confidence. But you must do it in half a second! Buy time – even if it is only for a few moments. Be calm, controlled and centred. Focus on the 3 C's:

- **Clarity**

Ask yourself: "What are the real results I want to achieve in this situation?" Be crystal clear on your goal.

- **Creativity**

Ask yourself: "What are the possible creative solutions? What are the consequences of each option? Which route do I want to follow?"

- **Concrete results**

Depending on the situation, do whatever you can to deliver concrete results.

The Strengths Toolbox

Sounds simple in theory, but it can be difficult in practice. The key is to be calm, buy time and consider your options. Try tackling the following exercise. Think of a situation where you want to flow. Then explore how you can channel your energy in a positive way – even after experiencing a setback. Rehearse until you feel ready to enter the arena. Then be fully present and do your best to reach the goal. Sometimes it will work, sometimes it won't – but it is vital to be true to yourself. You are then more likely to flow, rather than freeze.

The specific situation in which I want to flow is:

* ....

The things I can do to rehearse so that I can flow in the situation are:

* ....
* ....
* ....

The things I can do to flow when I am in the situation are:

* ....
* ....
* ....

The things I can do to recover after setbacks and continue to flow in the situation are:

* ....
* ....
* ....

3 tips for being real in your role

People sometimes go through three stages during their professional career. First, they begin by being real. Second, they became wrapped in playing a professional role. Third, they are real in their professional role. Let's explore these three steps.

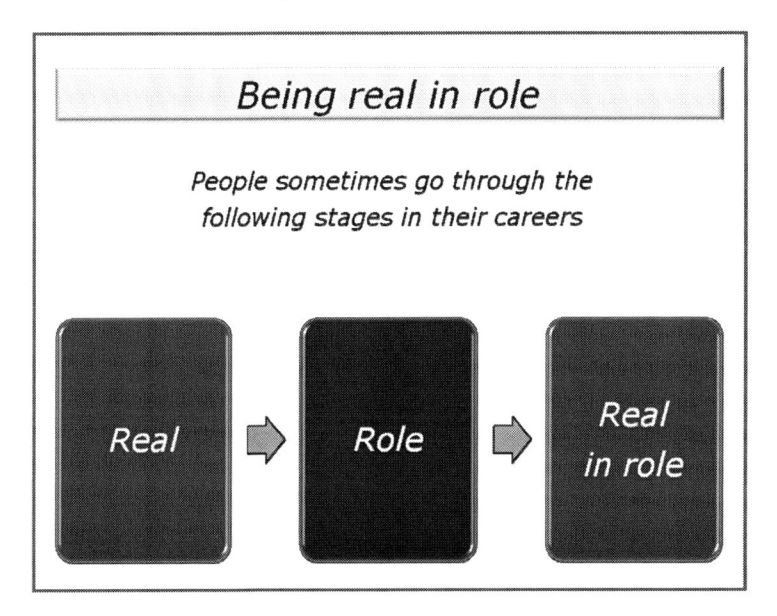

Being real in role

People sometimes go through the following stages in their careers

Real → Role → Real in role

1) Being real.

People often show passion when starting out on their chosen career. They are real, raw and may be classified as a 'rough diamond'. Throwing themselves into their work, they sometimes make mistakes – but this is part of the adventure. Their spark transmits energy and fire. Singer-songwriters, for example, sometimes produce great work early in their careers. Belying their youth, they write songs that convey wisdom beyond their years. The same happens in many fields. Stoked by idealism, people look forward to going to work each day – then comes the next stage.

2) *Being in role.*

People may climb the career ladder and, at a certain point, feel they must get into 'role'. Certainly they must be professional – but sometimes they bury their personality and become wrapped in the role. This may manifest itself by, for example, losing touch with customers, collecting 'badges', talking in long sentences, making things complicated or whatever. "I stopped doing what I do best," said one person, "and spent my life acting as a middle management supervisor. Two years into the job I felt confident enough to begin showing my real personality." This brings us to the next stage.

3) *Being real in role.*

Confident in their professional ability, they are real yet also able to fulfil their role. Great leaders, for example, show the 'human touch'. They feel more able to 'be themselves' and, far from diminishing their authority, this increases their credibility. How can you continue to be real in your role? Three principles are worth bearing in mind. First, be passionate. Do things you feel passionately about and let your passion shine through. Second, be professional. Fulfil your professional obligations – and do these superbly. Third, be a peak performer. Do something special that adds that touch of magic. Try completing the following sentence.

The things I can do to continue be real in my role are:

* ....
* ....
* ....

3 tips for finishing

Finishing is a key skill in life. "Flow, focus, finish and, as a by-product, find fulfilment," is the motto. Sounds easy in theory, but how does it work in practice? For example, how can you complete a book, perform well to the final whistle in a sporting event or finish a project successfully? Here are three tips for finishing.

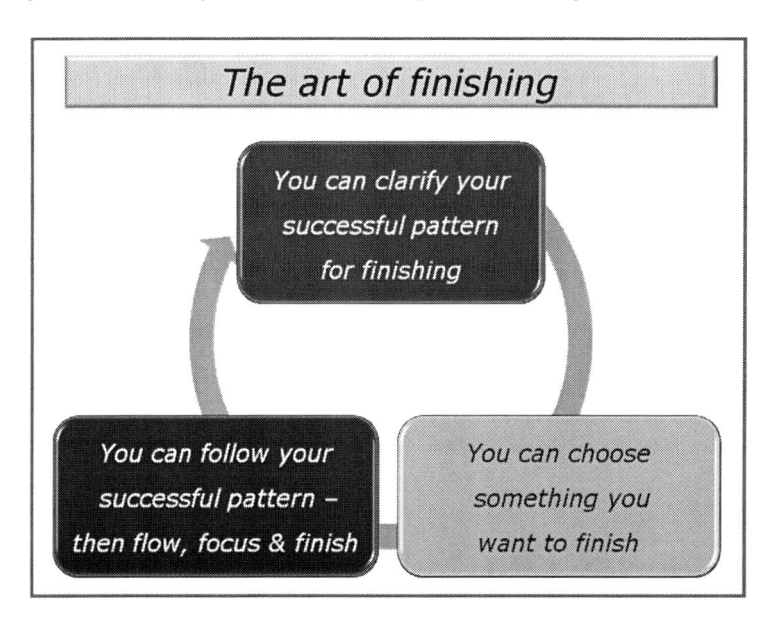

The art of finishing

- You can clarify your successful pattern for finishing
- You can choose something you want to finish
- You can follow your successful pattern – then flow, focus & finish

1) *You can clarify your successful pattern for finishing.*

Try tackling the exercise called *Finishing*. Looking back at your life, describe something you have finished successfully. What did you do right then? Be super specific. For example, one person said:

"Five years ago I finally completed work on refurbishing the 'Granny annexe' at our house, something I had delayed for years. First, I decided whether or not I wanted to do it. Certainly I could have hired a local builder – which would have freed up time – but I

The Strengths Toolbox

chose to finish it myself. Second, I set aside time to do the job, booking long weekends over a period of 12 months. I ringfenced this time, rather than allowing it to become cluttered by other events."

"Third, I established a working ritual, starting on Friday morning, working all day and most of Saturday, then allocating the rest of the weekend to the family. Fourth, I made it as pleasurable as possible, playing my favourite music, listening to the radio and having frequent coffee breaks. Fifth, I followed the discipline and kept working until it was finished. Now my teenage kids have moved into that part of the house – so Granny will have to wait."

Clarify your successful pattern for finishing. Consider how you can follow similar principles in the future. There may also be other strategies and skills you can add to be an even better finisher. (You may have different patterns in your personal and professional life. For example, when moving on from a relationship or completing a work project.) Try completing the exercise on this theme – then go onto the next step.

The time I finished something successfully was:

* ....

The specific things I did to finish it successfully were:

* ....

* ....

* ....

The steps I can take to finish things successfully in the future are:

* ....

* ....

* ....

2) You can choose something you want to finish.

Looking into the future, choose something you want to finish. Be selective to be effective. You can't complete everything in life. Providing you accept the consequences, it can be okay to say: "I don't want to finish it." Then focus on other priorities. Identify what you want to finish and treat it like a 'project'. Employ good planning exercises. For example, start by clarifying your picture of perfection. Identify the pluses and minuses involved in reaching the goal – and decide whether you want to go for it. If so, clarify the three things you can do to give yourself the greatest chance of success. Create a road map – a project plan – for achieving the picture of perfection. Try completing the following sentence.

The specific thing I would like to finish in the future is:

* ....

3) You can follow your successful pattern – then flow, focus and finish.

Set aside time to finish, otherwise you are destined to fail. Divide the task into reasonable chunks and set yourself a realistic goal for each time period. Reaching it will give you a sense of achievement. The next step is to follow your successful pattern – or a pattern you know works for finishing.

"One of the hardest challenges I faced was getting my players to finish properly," said one football manager. "Many were extremely talented but had a habit of falling at the final hurdle. Frequently they got ahead in games, only to collapse in the last 15 minutes. Going into a state of paralysis, they began looking at the clock, retreating into their half and kicking the ball anywhere, rather than playing football. They needed to develop good habits.

"I got them to 'look beyond' the finishing line. They needed to assume the game would last 100 minutes and keep playing football. They went back to basics: win the ball, pass the ball – move, move, move. The team must keep its 'shape' – but the key was psychological. People needed to play the positive game – plus some

The Strengths Toolbox

of the 'percentage' game – rather than lapse into the paralysis game. Fortunately they got into the habit of winning matches by playing football for 100 minutes – rather than playing for 75 and retiring to the rocking chair. The players become good finishers and went on to win trophies."

You will have your own way of finishing, but here are some suggestions. Make good use of your prime times – the times when you have most energy. Eat properly, take time to relax, rest and recover. Encourage yourself. Surround yourself with positive things – people, music or whatever. Everybody experiences setbacks. When you hit difficulties, lift your eyes to focus on the picture of perfection. See things in perspective. If possible, learn to love the process as much as reaching the prize.

Do the right things in the right way every day. Be calm, controlled and centred. Keep working hard – then flow, focus and finish. After completing the task, it is time to relax and reflect. Clarify what you did well – and how you can do more of these things in the future. Clarify what you can do even better next time – and how. Try completing the following sentence.

The specific things I can do to flow, focus and finish are:

* ....
* ....
* ....

Finishing is just another name for beginning. Soon it will be time to find another challenge to tackle, another dream to pursue. You can then again follow your successful pattern for finishing. Enjoy the journey.

3 tips for managing crises successfully

How can you manage crises successfully? One approach is to focus on calmness, clarify and concrete results. Let's explore how you can follow these steps in your own way.

Managing crises successfully

You can focus on:

- Calmness
- Clarity
- Concrete results

1) You can focus on calmness.

Calmness is crucial – whether you are arriving at the scene of an accident, solving a customer problem, counselling a distressed person or whatever. It is vital to 'buy time'. You need to get an overview of the situation, clarify the key challenges and focus on the result you want to achieve. Sometimes you may also need to transmit calmness to other people. How can you apply this approach in your own way? Start by thinking of a challenging situation that you may face in the future. You may suffer a setback at work, face a

The Strengths Toolbox

difficult illness, experience a crisis in a relationship or whatever. How can you stay composed? How can you buy time? How can you see things in perspective? Try completing the following sentence.

The specific things I can do to stay calm in the challenging situation are:

* ....

* ....

* ....

2) You can focus on clarity.

Clarity is vital is two areas – the 'What' and the 'How'. You need to clarify what you aim to achieve and how you aim to achieve it. Let's explore these two stages.

You can clarify the 'What'.

Whilst you may need to act quickly, your actions must – as far as possible – fit in with the longer-term goal. So begin by asking yourself: "What are the real results I want to achieve? What is the picture of perfection?"

Imagine you are a doctor arriving at the scene of a motorway accident. Certainly you may need to act quickly to save lives – but you must also bear in mind the long-term effects. Pulling a person clear may release them quickly, but it may also cause other damage. You want them to regain their health and be able to walk again. What is the real result you want to achieve – both long-term and short-term? Let's consider another situation. Imagine you are having an argument with your partner. What is the real goal you want to achieve? Do you want to win the present argument or build a long-term 'win-win' relationship?

Establishing the real 'What' will influence 'How' you tackle the situation. You may, of course, have a mixture of short, medium and long-term goals. If so, brainstorm all the things you want to achieve, list these in order of priority – then focus on tackling them from the

Strengths

top down. Looking at the critical situation you may face in the future, try completing the following sentence.

The specific things I can do to clarify the 'What' – the real results I want to achieve – in the challenging situation are:

* ....

* ....

* ....

You can clarify the 'How'.

Let's move onto the 'How' – the strategy for achieving the goals. Bearing in mind the results you want to achieve, begin by exploring the potential solutions. You can do this by going through three stages.

- **You can focus on 'controlling the controllables'.**

People like to feel in charge. So begin by asking yourself: "What are the things I can control in the situation? What are the things I can't control? How can I build on what I can control and manage what I can't."

- **You can focus on the 'choices, consequences and creative solutions'.**

Ask yourself: "What are the choices – the various options – in this situation? What are the consequences – the pluses and minuses – of each option? What are the potential creative solutions? For example, what are the best parts of each option? Can I put these together to create another solution? Are there any other imaginative solutions?"

- **You can focus on the 'conclusions'.**

Make a decision. Looking at all the possible options, ask yourself: "Which route do I want to take? How can I build on the pluses and minimise the minuses?" Choose your way forward. (Sometimes, of course, you may try several parallel strategies.) Looking at a critical

The Strengths Toolbox

situation you may face in the future, try completing the following sentence.

The specific things I can do to clarify the 'How' – the strategy for moving forward in the challenging situation – are:

* ....
* ....
* ....

3) *You can focus on concrete results.*

Commit to your chosen strategy. Work hard, concentrate fully and, if appropriate, get some early wins. Encourage yourself and other people. Keep going until you deliver the required concrete results. Looking ahead to the possible critical situation you may face in the future, try completing the following sentence.

The specific things I can do to work hard to deliver concrete results in the challenging situation are:

* ....
* ....
* ....

Good crisis managers then look beyond the present. After solving the problem, they take learn lessons and identify areas for improvement. Ask yourself: "What can I learn from the crisis? How can I prevent the problem happening again in the future? If it does occur again, however, how can I manage similar situations better in the future?" Clarify your conclusions – then put your action plans in place. Good crisis management can be the trigger for improving your quality of life in the future.

3 tips for recognising that 'what you focus on, you become'

"Study success," said one of my teachers. "You are then more likely to feel optimistic. Study cynicism and you are more likely to be cynical. That does not mean you should ignore reality. Study solutions, however, rather than constantly analyse failure. What you focus on, you become."

What you study – or put into your system – has an effect on how you feel. This is the law of return. Let's explore how you can focus on what you want to become.

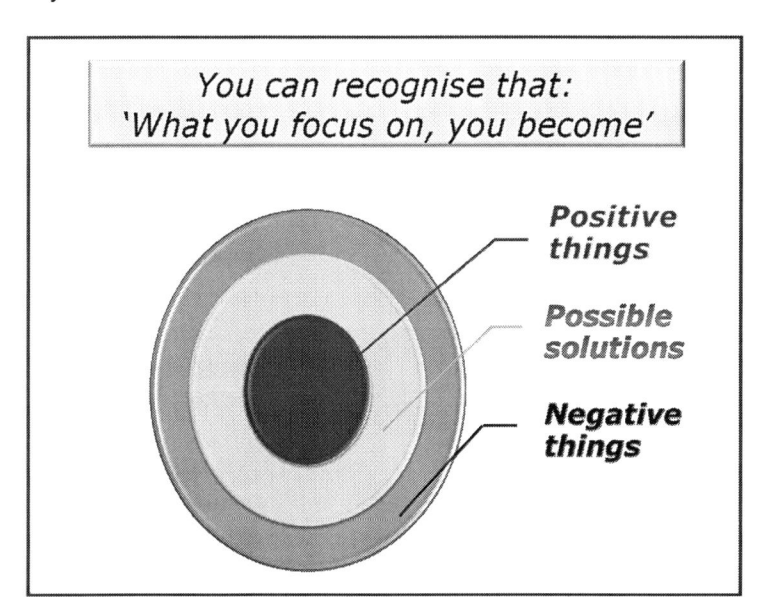

You can recognise that:
'What you focus on, you become'

- **Positive things**
- **Possible solutions**
- **Negative things**

1) *You can clarify what you focus on.*

What is your natural approach? Do you focus on things that are positive or negative? Do you concentrate on beauty or ugliness; solutions or problems; hope or despair? Do you count your blessings

The Strengths Toolbox

or worry about what is missing? Do you spend time with people who are creative or those who complain?

Martin Seligman, a renowned psychologist, describes his own 'Road To Damascus' moment when his 8-year-old daughter said to him, in effect: "Dad, I might do much better if you occasionally told me what I did well." He went on to write books such as *Learned Optimism*. Until recently, he maintains, psychologists could only get funding if they studied how people became 'ill'. So they became experts in pointing out how people failed. He is now trying to reverse that trend and founded The Positive Psychology Network. So what do you focus on? Try completing the following sentence.

The things I focus on now are:

* ....
* ....
* ....

2) *You can clarify what you want to focus on.*

Depending on which society you live in, you may be assailed by negative messages through the media. The constant argument, criticism and carping can take its toll. Yes, it is vital to see challenges and find creative solutions – but you need positive energy to make that happen.

"Ten years ago I changed dramatically," said one person. "Being a 'caring parent', I wanted my children to grow up happily. But then one day I got a shock. My son asked me: 'Is the world going to end?' My answer was, 'Of course not,' but I wanted to know why he asked the question. He had been looking at my doom and gloom environmental magazines – a mood that I sometimes expressed when friends were round for dinner. Suddenly I took notice. I wanted to build a happier, more sustainable world, but I was poisoning my own home. Now I take magazines that show practical ways we can improve the world – rather than those that fill people with despair. It was a tough lesson."

Strengths

What do you want to focus on? You may want to spend more time encouraging other people, playing music, enjoying the arts, caring for your garden, creating beauty or whatever. Describe what you would like to spend your energy concentrating on – and how you can take steps to make that happen. Try completing the following sentences.

The things I want to focus on in the future are:

* ....
* ....
* ....

The steps I can take to focus on these things are:

* ....
* ....
* ....

3) *You can become more like what you focus on.*

This is a challenge and calls for developing positive habits. You may remember the old story about Gandhi.

One day a mother brought her son to see the great man and said: 'Can you please tell him to stop eating sugar?" Gandhi asked them to come back in 2 weeks. The date duly arrived and Gandhi told the boy to stop eating sugar. The mother thanked him but, before leaving, she asked: "Why couldn't you tell him that two weeks ago?" His answer was: "I had to give up sugar first." Gandhi believed you had to 'be' the message.

Let's imagine that you develop your chosen habits. What will be the results of focusing on what you want to become? Try completing the following sentence.

The Strengths Toolbox

The benefits of doing this will be:

* ....
* ....
* ....

3 tips for making good use of the fallow times

"I often experience a sense of flow in my work, such as when doing a rewarding project," said one person. "But after completing the job I sometimes go into the doldrums. It's obviously because I have lost the sense of purpose I had when doing the task. Wanting to fill the vacuum, I am tempted to jump into the next project, even though it may not be too stimulating. How can I recapture that sense of purpose?"

Peak performers learn how to use the 'fallow' times. These are the hours, days and months that come between feeling frustrated and enjoying a sense of flow. Making good use of these times can help to shape your creative future. Let's explore three steps for making this happen.

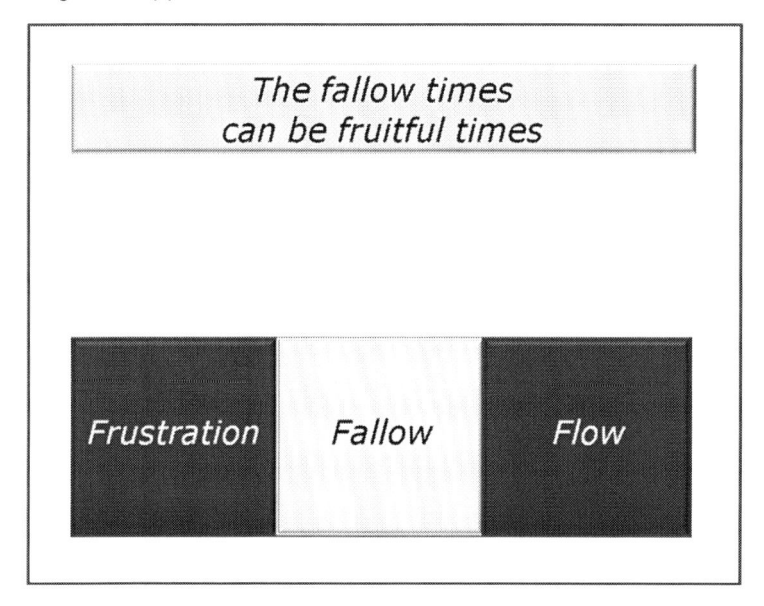

The fallow times can be fruitful times

| Frustration | Fallow | Flow |

1) You can recognise the importance of the fallow times.

People love to experience what Mihaly Csikszentmihalyi called 'a sense of flow'. When you are doing something stimulating, you feel stretched and 'time seems to go away'. Reaching your goal is satisfying – but afterwards you may feel frustrated. You want to climb the next mountain, pursue the next adventure or whatever. It is then useful to remember the agricultural tradition of allowing a field to lie fallow. The pasture can rest, recover and become revitalised. Creative artists also know the value of 'giving themselves permission' to be fallow. Providing these are used properly, fallow times can be fruitful times. The first step is to recognise and capitalise on these periods. How can this work for you? Try completing the following sentence.

The things I can do to recognise the fallow times and then give myself permission to be fallow are:

* ....

* ....

* ....

2) You can make good use of the fallow times.

"During the fallow times I surround myself with positive things," said one person. "Getting up in the morning, I play my favourite music. This provides a stimulating start to the day, rather than listening to politicians arguing on the radio. I spend time with friends who give me energy, rather than negative people. 'Everything is food', say the Zen Buddhists, so I control what I allow into my body. Because I am in a vacuum, I must set the agenda – even if it means choosing to 'do nothing' – rather than allow others to set the agenda. Surrounding myself with positive influences means I am eventually more likely to find a meaningful purpose."

How can you make good use of such times? You do not need to put everything 'on hold'. One approach is to continue working at the 'day job' – whilst also gathering information about possible future challenges. At the same time, however, it is vital to surround yourself with positive influences. Try completing the following sentence.

The things I can do to make good use of the fallow times are:

* ....
* ....
* ....

3) You can recognise when it is time to move on from being fallow and go into flow.

Providing you do the right things, eventually a stimulating 'project' will emerge. How will you know it if it right to move? Ask yourself: "Does this contribute to achieving my personal or professional goals? Does thinking about it give me positive energy? Will pursuing it give me a sense of fulfilment?" If the answers are "Yes," seize the opportunity. If you are not absolutely sure, but feel tempted to spring back into action, make sure it is a challenge you respect. Otherwise, like a mountaineer who does not respect the mountain, you may suffer a catastrophe. Making good use of the fallow times means you are more likely to choose the right project. Embarking on the adventure, you can then flow, focus and finish. Try completing the following sentence.

The things I can do to recognise when it is time to move on from being fallow and go into flow are:

* ....
* ....
* ....

3 tips for getting positive energy

Energy is life. So what gives you positive energy? What gives you negative energy? How can you get more positive energy in the future? You may then be able to give even more to other people. Let's explore three steps for making this happen.

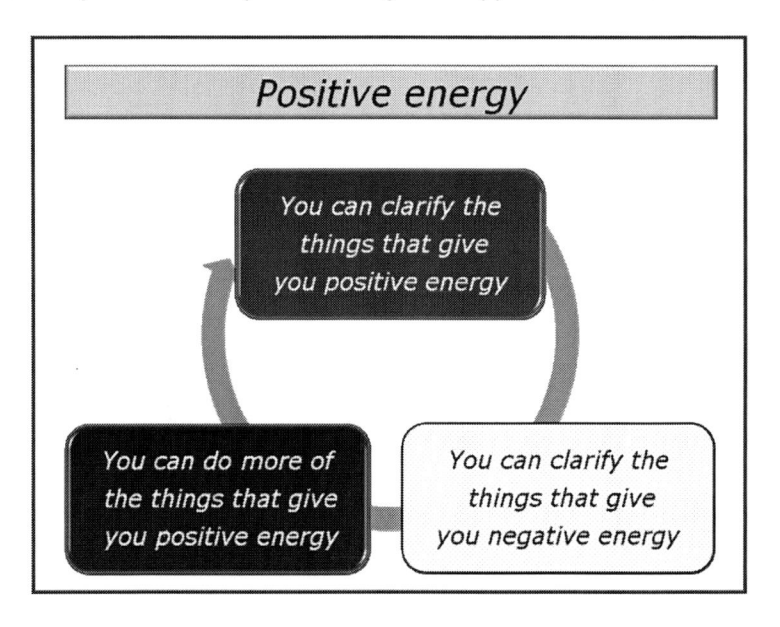

Positive energy

- You can clarify the things that give you positive energy
- You can clarify the things that give you negative energy
- You can do more of the things that give you positive energy

1) You can clarify the things that give you positive energy.

Start by describing the things you find stimulating. For example, the people, projects and pleasures that put a spring into your step. Later we will look at how you can do more of these things in the future.

People who are 'Givers' sometimes find it hard to give to themselves. Sheila Cassidy is such a 'Giver'. During the 1970s she was imprisoned in Chile for providing medical care to opponents of the Pinochet regime. Returning to the UK after being tortured, she went on to become Medical Director of St Luke's Hospice in

Strengths

Plymouth. Sheila gave to others, but starved herself of pleasures. Hard work took its toll, however, and she began taking more care of herself. Writing in her book *Sharing The Darkness*, Sheila explains:

"Perhaps the final fall from my self-styled perch of grace came at the beginning of the winter season when *Brideshead Revisited* was serialised for television. Until then I had stalwartly refused to have more than a transistor radio and tape recorder, but now I could bear it no longer and rushed into town to buy myself a TV."

Sheila found that, far from corrupting her contribution, she gave even more to other people. Try completing the follow exercise.

The things that give me positive energy are:

* ....
* ....
* ....

2) You can clarify the things that give you negative energy.

Stimulation is crucial – but sometimes it can also be good to identify what saps your energy. Describe things you find draining, such as serial complainers, 'observer critics' or whatever. Try completing the following exercise.

The things that give me negative energy are:

* ....
* ....
* ....

3) You can do more of the things that give you positive energy.

"Nowadays I spend more time with encouragers," said one person.

The Strengths Toolbox

"They help me to feel more real, more myself. Music also lifts my soul. So now I start the day with upbeat music, rather than listening to bad news on the radio. During my twenties I became so depressed that I made Eeyore look cheerful. Certainly I keep abreast of current events, but now I focus on doing what I can to improve the world."

Looking to the future, you may want to consider two things. First, do more of the things that are inspiring. Second, stop doing some of the things that are draining. Try combining these elements to complete the following exercise.

The steps I can take to do more of the things that give me positive energy are:

* ....
* ....
* ....

People can choose their attitude. They can choose to be givers or takers, creators or complainers, encouragers or stoppers. Givers also need encouragement, however, so it is important to keep getting positive energy. You will then have even more encouragement to give to other people.

3 tips for getting a 'perfect ten'

Peter Vidmar won a gymnastics Gold Medal at the 1984 Los Angeles Olympics. Looking back at how his event was scored in those days, he describes the steps people took to score the 'perfect 10', which was first achieved by Nadia Comaneci in Montreal. Firstly, they must achieve the Olympic standard of technical competence. This often took years of dedication and would give them the 9.4. They could then add 0.2 by taking a risk; 0.2 by demonstrating originality – something that had never been done before; and 0.2 by showing virtuosity – flair. Such a brilliant performance would produce the Perfect 10 and, hopefully, the Olympic Gold.

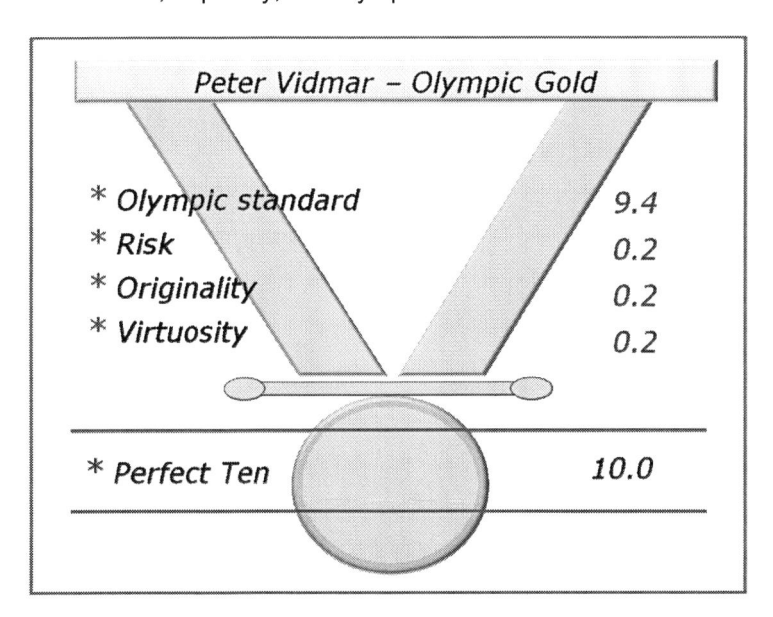

Peter Vidmar – Olympic Gold

* Olympic standard	9.4
* Risk	0.2
* Originality	0.2
* Virtuosity	0.2
* Perfect Ten	10.0

Peter is a 'class act' who now makes his living as an inspiring speaker. Many people leave his sessions fired up. Some say: "We can now believe in our dreams. All we have to do is to be original, take risks and demonstrate virtuosity." They only forget one thing. Peter's most important message is that people must first achieve the 9.4. That

The Strengths Toolbox

is the first step towards winning an Olympic Gold. Here are three tips for following these steps in your own way.

1) You can start by choosing an activity in which you stand a chance of achieving the 9.4.

You will obviously start by playing to your strengths. Focus on a *specific activity* in which: a) You get positive energy; b) You stand a chance of delivering peak performance. What is your professional version of the Olympics? Which is the 'event' in which you can win a 'gold medal'? On the other hand, you may not be interested in 'competition'. You may be a pioneer who 'invents' a new event. Great performers are, by definition, extremists. They are extremely good at what they do. In the business world, for example, they are often brilliant niche suppliers. So focus on the activity in which you are in your element. You are at ease and yet excel. There is no point in going into an event where, at best, you can only get a 6/10. Try completing the following sentence.

The specific activity in which I stand a chance of achieving the 9.4 is:

* ....

2) You can work hard to achieve the 9.4.

Class acts build on their strengths. They are also prepared to sweat. They pursue the right strategy, find solutions to problems and work hard to achieve success. How can you pursue this path in your own way? Clarify your picture of perfection – the 'What' – then clarify the 'How'. Focus on: "The 3 key things I can do to give myself the greatest chance of success are: 1) ____ 2) ____ 3) ____" Settle on your road map – complete with milestones – then break it down into specific actions. Develop a daily disciplines. Start each day with an early success, encourage yourself on the journey and practise. 'Practise until you can forget'. Keep doing the right things in the right way until they become second nature. Do everything possible to reach your equivalent of the 9.4. Try completing the following sentence.

Strengths

The specific things I can do to work hard and reach my equivalent of the 9.4 are:

* ....
* ....
* ....

3) You can add the risk, originality and virtuosity to achieve the perfect 10.

Class acts deliver the goods at vital moments. Providing the foundation is in place, they may take what appears to be a risk. But in their minds – or in their muscle memory – they have done it a thousand times. One person said: "People say that I take risks, but I have already rehearsed all the scenarios, explored the possible strategies and settled on the way forward. I feel comfortable with what I am doing. In fact, it would be a greater risk not to take what appears to be a risk." Great performers also do something that appears original. But it is the result spending hours, days or months finding creative solutions to challenges. Then comes the final piece – virtuosity, flair or showmanship. Class acts add that 'touch of class'. They do something magical that stays in people's minds forever. How can you follow these steps in you own way? How can you build on the 9.4 and try to produce your equivalent of the 'perfect 10'? Try completing the following sentence.

The specific things I can do to build on the 9.4 and try to produce my equivalent of the 'perfect 10' are:

* ....
* ....
* ....

Peter Vidmar's approach is well worth exploring and you can read more about it in his book called *Risk, Originality & Virtuosity.*

3 tips for surfing the sigmoid curve

"My greatest challenge has been judging how long to stay in a particular role," said one person. "Looking back at my career, sometimes I kept growing – but other times I stayed too long. The danger has been lapsing into cruise control, when really I should have taken the next step in my career."

How can you decide when to stay or when to move? One approach is to 'surf the sigmoid curves'. (Originally a mathematical term, Charles Handy popularised the 'sigmoid curve' in his book *The Age of Paradox*. It is now used to chart the lifecycle of a person's development, an organisation, a product or even a civilisation.) As one curve reaches its zenith, you surf onto the next one, rather than sink into decline. Let's explore how to make this happen.

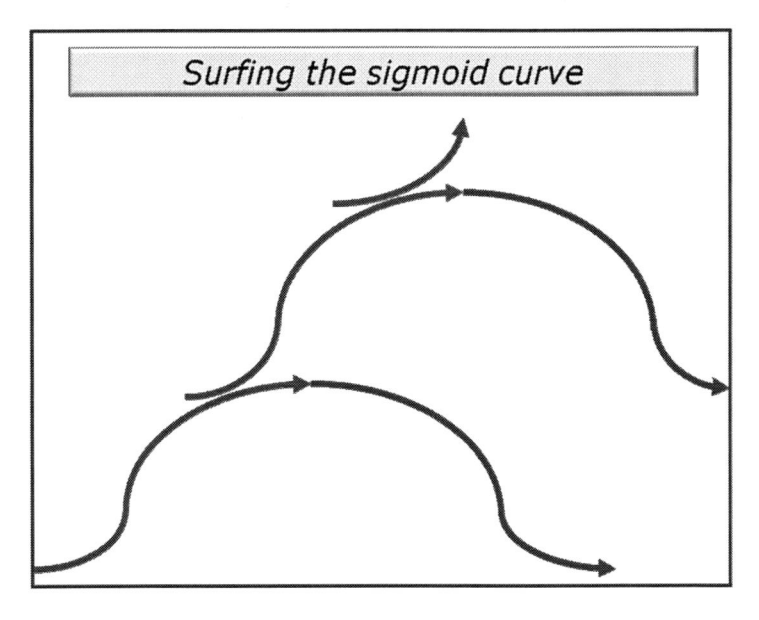

Surfing the sigmoid curve

Strengths

1) You can recognise where you are on the sigmoid curve.

Imagine you are climbing the curve in your professional life. Where are you now? (You may find it useful to focus on a specific aspect of your professional life.) Perhaps you are halfway up the curve. Feeling hungry, you may believe there is lots of scope for development. On the other hand, you may have hit a ceiling or believe the 'product' or service you offer is deteriorating. Looking at your professional life – or a particular aspect of it – chart where you are on the curve. Try completing the following sentence.

The place where I feel I am now on the sigmoid curve is:

* ....

2) You can go to the top of the sigmoid curve – but be aware of the warning signs.

How can you keep developing? How can you stay close to your customers? How can you help them to succeed? How can you keep improving your offering? How can you keep developing your 'A' talent? Let's look at the total picture. Do you feel at the top of the sigmoid curve? Can you see further growth ahead? Or are you beginning to get warning signs? If so, what are the symptoms? Keep going until you feel at the top of the curve. Try completing the following sentence.

The specific things I can do to keep developing and go to the top of the sigmoid curve are:

* ....
* ....
* ....

The Strengths Toolbox

3) You can surf onto the next sigmoid curve.

Where is your own energy going? What do find exciting? How can you do more of these things? Looking at your chosen field, what will be happening in the next 5 years? What will be the key challenges your customers will be facing? How can you help them to succeed? How can you stay ahead of the game? How can you surf onto the next sigmoid curve? Perhaps you can even create one. Try completing the following sentence.

The specific things I can do to surf onto the next sigmoid curve are:

* ....
* ....
* ....

3 tips for spring-cleaning your life

Sometimes it is important to have a 'Spring-clean' to sort–out our lives. Clutter absorbs energy. So it is useful to refocus on the things that are really important. Try tackling *The white room* exercise.

The white room exercise

Imagine your life is a 'white room'. There is nothing in it except your family. You are then invited to do the following things. You can put:

* *3 people into your room.*

* *3 strengths & 3 goals in your room.*

* *3 possessions & 3 other things in your room.*

Describe what you would put in your white room.

---

1) You can put 3 people in your white room.

"Two people immediately came to mind – my best friend and my partner at work," said one person. "But the next stage was much harder. Which person should I put in the room? It was a bit like *Desert Island Discs*, but more serious. Eventually I chose one person – but that was not really the point. The exercise forced me to think about: a) The people with whom I feel alive; b) The people who it would good to meet occasionally; c) The people with whom there was no longer a 'click'. I decided to spend more time with the people who lifted my spirits."

The Strengths Toolbox

Who would you put in your room? Try completing the following sentence.

The three people I would put into my room would be:

* ....

* ....

* ....

2) You can put 3 strengths and 3 goals into your white room.

Ask yourself: "What do I find most fulfilling? What are the 3 things I do best? What are the activities in which I flow, focus and finish?" Put your top 3 strengths into the room. Then clarify your goals. Ask yourself: "What is my picture of success? Looking back when I am 80, what for me will mean I have had a successful life? What are my personal and professional goals?" Put your top 3 goals into the room. Later you can make an action plan for achieving this picture of success. Try completing the following sentences.

The three strengths I would put into my room would be:

* ....

* ....

* ....

The three goals I would put into my room would be:

* ....

* ....

* ....

Strengths

3) You can put 3 possessions and 3 other things into your white room.

Time to treat yourself. List the 3 possessions you want to put into the room. One person found a 'creative' way around this, saying: "Assuming I am allowed to put in my home and pets, I would put in my computer, TV and car. But I would also have a good clear-out. We have so much stuff in the house and garage that we never use. Just looking at it takes energy. Regarding the 3 other things, I would include my mountaineering equipment, camera and painting materials." So what possessions would you put in the room? Plus what would be the 3 other things? So now you have your family plus 15 items – people, strengths, goals, possessions, other things – into your new life. Try completing the following sentences.

The three possessions I would put into my room would be:

* ....

* ....

* ....

The three other things I would put into my room would be:

* ....

* ....

* ....

The white room exercise sounds drastic. But sometimes we need to refocus our lives. We can then concentrate on the people and activities that give us positive energy. Don't worry. Clutter will soon appear – and then it will be time for a new spring-clean.

3 tips for creating perfect days

Eugene O'Kelly was the CEO of the accountant firm KPMG when he got the news. Writing in *Chasing Daylight*, the then 53 year-old explains how the message transformed his life. He says: "I was blessed. I was told I had three months to live." Eugene decided to live the way he wanted to live. Tearing up his diary, he aimed to create perfect moments, perfect hours and perfect days. Dramatic events can shake our foundations, but we can often be more proactive in shaping our personal and professional lives. Here are three suggestions for creating perfect days.

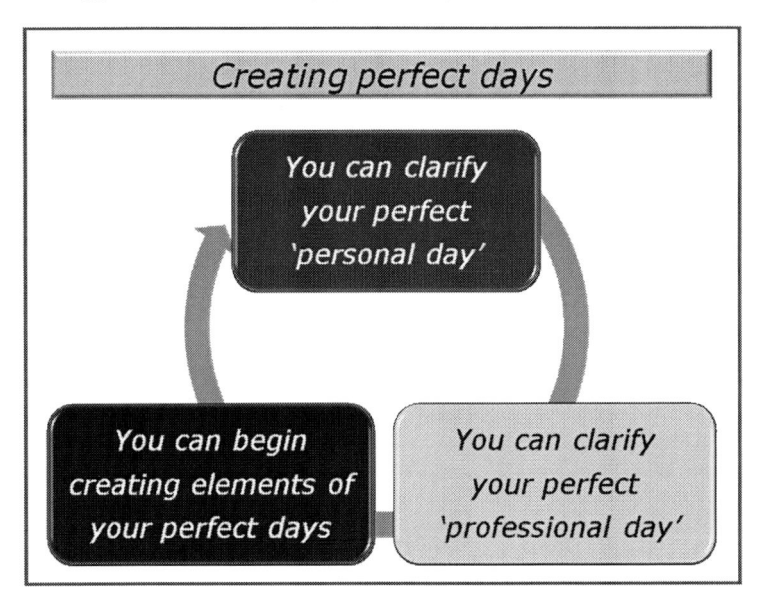

Creating perfect days

- You can clarify your perfect 'personal day'
- You can clarify your perfect 'professional day'
- You can begin creating elements of your perfect days

1) You can clarify your perfect 'personal day'.

Try tackling the exercise on this theme. Start by brainstorming and then crafting your perfect 'personal day'. Different people will obviously have different days. For example, you may start with a leisurely breakfast; go for a run; spend time with your children; work in the garden; listen to music; paint, write or do some other creative activity; enjoy a siesta; or whatever. You may also have several different kinds of perfect days.

My perfect 'personal day' would be to:

* ....
* ....
* ....

2) You can clarify your perfect 'professional day'.

Continue by brainstorming and then crafting your perfect 'professional day' – the way you can earn money. For example, you may use your 'A' talent; throw yourself into a stimulating project; be with stimulating people; work in a stimulating place – culture and environment; gain great satisfaction; see an end product; or whatever. Again, you may have several different kinds of perfect professional days. Sometimes your ideal personal and professional days may be blended together.

My perfect 'professional day' would be to:

* ....
* ....
* ....

3) You can begin creating elements of your perfect days.

"Everything is temporary, nothing is permanent," we are told. Eugene O'Kelly understood this message. His book is subtitled: "How my forthcoming death transformed my life." So he began creating his perfect days. We can each follow this path in our own lives.

The Strengths Toolbox

Looking ahead, consider how you can introduce parts of your 'perfect days' into your personal and professional life. Begin by putting in a few elements – then start to join these together like a row of pearls. Life is for living and Eugene O'Kelly reminds us to live life. Perfection may not be attainable and things may not always work out – but then each day may be 'perfect with its imperfections'.

The steps I can take to begin creating elements of my perfect days are:

* ....
* ....
* ....

Super teams

3 tips for building a super team

Super teams are special. They have a compelling purpose and translate this into a clear picture of perfection. People choose to opt into the team and make their best contribution towards achieving the goals. They do professional work, solve problems and deliver peak performance. People then do everything possible to achieve the picture of perfection.

The super teams approach comes with three health warnings. First, it works. Second, it looks simple on paper, but does not mean it is easy. Third, it calls for taking tough decisions, especially about people. There are normally seven steps towards building such a team – see illustration – but we can break these down into three main stages.

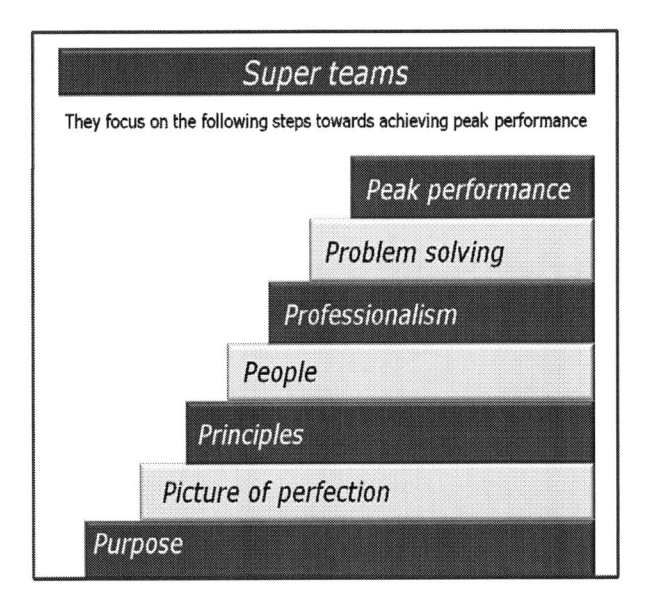

Super teams

They focus on the following steps towards achieving peak performance

- Peak performance
- Problem solving
- Professionalism
- People
- Principles
- Picture of perfection
- Purpose

1) You can clarify the purpose, picture of perfection and principles.

Start by creating a compelling purpose. This is the team's reason for being – the 'What'. Translate the purpose into a clear picture of perfection. (You can find more details about how to create this picture in next piece in the *Toolbox*.) Pick a date in the future. Describe the actual things that will be happening then that will show the team has reached its goal. If possible, produce an inspiring 'one-liner' that sums up your aim. Draw a road map towards achieving the target. Start from your destination and work backwards. Describe the milestones – the specific things the team must achieve at each stage of the journey. Describe the 'actual words' you want to hear different groups of people saying along the way.

After clarifying the 'What', revisit the 'Why'. Clarify the benefits of reaching the goals – for the organisation, the customers and the team members. Move onto the 'How'. Clarify the key principles – the key strategies – the team can follow to give it the greatest chance of success. You are now ready to communicate the purpose, picture of perfection and principles – but then comes the crucial step.

2) You can get the right people.

Get the right people with the right spirit – because otherwise you are sunk. Great teams are built on 'similarity of spirit and diversity of strengths'. Diversity of spirit is a recipe for disaster. Get the right balance between 'soul players' and 'star players'. Soul players embody the spirit of the team. They are consistent players who do the right things every day. Star players also embody the spirit, but they also add 'little bit extra'. There is no place for 'semi-detached' players who are waiting to be motivated. One negative person can dilute the energy of many people in the team.

Clear contracting is crucial and is the hallmark of healthy cultures. There are three things you can do to make this happen. First, communicate the picture of perfection. Second, invite people to proactively get back to you to show how they want to contribute to achieving the picture of perfection. Third, bearing in mind each person's strengths, make clear contracts about their part in reaching the goals. (You can find out more about this process in the piece called *3 tips for clarifying each person's contribution to the picture of perfection.*)

"But in his book *Good to Great*, Jim Collins says get the people first," somebody may say. Jim Collins has written a tremendous book, but on this point he is sometimes misunderstood. When hiring people, it is vital to know roughly the kind of business in which you aim to achieve peak performance. If you are in the alpine climbing business, for example, hire people who have a passion for alpine climbing. Otherwise you may collect rock climbers, free climbers and scuba divers who have different agendas. Clarify the kind of 'mountain' you are climbing, then give people empowerment – within parameters – to finalise the goals and implement their part of the strategy.

3) You can enable people to be professional, solve problems and achieve peak performance.

Great teams develop good habits. They keep doing the right things in the right way every day. Invite each person – or, in larger groups, each team – to describe the specific things they will do to deliver the goods. Ask them to proactively keep you informed about the actions they are taking to tackle the issues that are in the 'Green, Amber & Red' zones. Great teams contain resilient people who overcome setbacks. Educate them to stay calm during crises, solve problems and deliver the goods when it matters. Encourage people to keep working hard and achieve the picture of perfection.

You will probably have your own philosophy for building a great team. So try tackling the following exercise. First, describe a super team that you have admired. It can be one in sports, business, the arts or whatever. Second, describe what you think people did right to deliver success. Third, describe how you can follow these steps in your own way to build a super team.

The name of the super team is:

* ....

The things that people did right to deliver success were:

* ....

* ....

* ....

The specific things I can do to follow these steps in my own way to build a super team are:

* ....

* ....

* ....

One ending is a new beginning. Some teams disband after reaching the goal. Other teams refocus on the purpose and translate it into a new picture of perfection. Pacesetting teams, for example, have a special kind of psychology. They aim to take the lead, maintain the lead and extend the lead. Staying ahead of everybody else, they make the new rules for the game. Guiding your team to success, you may then want to repeat the process. As they say in sport: "First build a team, then a club, then a dynasty." This calls for making even tougher decisions on the road towards building a second generation super team.

3 tips for clarifying your team's picture of perfection

Super teams have a crystal clear goal. Everybody knows what mountain they are climbing, why they are climbing it and when they will reach the summit. Everybody also knows their part in achieving the goals.

1) You can clarify the picture of perfection.

Try tackling the exercise called *The picture of perfection* – see below. Start by defining the big 'What'. Pick a date in the future and define the goal you want the team to achieve by that date. Try to create a 'one-liner' that summarises the goal. Beneath this headline, describe the specific things that will be happening then that will show the team has reached the goal.

The Picture of Perfection

The 'What'

The goal we want to achieve by _____ is:

* To _____

The specific things that will be happening then that will show we have reached our goal will be:

* _____

* _____

* _____

Two points are worth mentioning concerning the 'one-liner' and making the big goal more concrete.

a) The 'one-liner'.

This should appeal to both the heart and the head. Don't expect the sentence to come easily. You may start with a rather bland goal – but can refine it in the future. Continue until you are satisfied with the one-liner.

b) The specific things that will show the team has reached the goal.

This is an attempt to break down the big goal to make it more specific. Businesses that clarify their picture of perfection, for example, often build it around the 3 P's: Profitability; Product quality – including service quality; and People. They describe the specific things that will be happening in these areas when the company reaches the goal. Some are now adding a fourth P: Planet. You will, of course, have your own sub-sections.

2) You can make a road map towards achieving the picture of perfection.

After clarifying the end goal, move onto the next stage. *Starting from the destination and working backwards,* make a road map of the milestones along the way. List the actual things the team will have achieved at each stage of the journey. Bring it to life by writing the *actual words* you want to hear specific people saying at each of the stages. For example, what do you want to hear your sponsors, customers and team members saying?

3) You can give your team a sense of ownership in completing the picture of perfection.

Set aside 2 hours to meet with your team. Describe the road towards achieving the picture of perfection – the POP. You can present this on Power Points, but transfer the main headings and dates to flip

The Strengths Toolbox

charts that can be laid out on the floor. Describe the benefits of achieving the goals and answer any questions they may have about the road map.

	The picture of perfection	
	The goal is:	
	To _____	
The date is:	The specific things we will have achieved by then will be:	The words we want to hear people saying then will be:
* _____	* _____	· _____
	* _____	· _____
	* _____	· _____
* _____	* _____	· _____
	* _____	· _____
	* _____	· _____
* _____	* _____	· _____
	* _____	· _____
	* _____	· _____

Then give people a chance to contribute to the POP. Give each person a pack of Post-it Notes. They have 10 minutes to write things they would like to see added to the road map. They are to write one idea per Post-it, but can compile as many ideas as they wish. Each person then goes up in turn and puts their suggestions on the relevant parts of the road map. They are also to explain what they have written on each Post-it. You will have the final call, of course, but it can be good to integrate some of these ideas into the POP. Set up another team session for a week or so later to present and 'sign off' the final version. Everybody will then know the road map towards achieving the team's picture of perfection.

3 tips for clarifying your team's strategies for success

Imagine you are a leader. You have clarified what mountain the team is climbing. Everybody is agreed on the end goal – the picture of perfection. This is the 'What'. You must now clarify the strategies for reaching the summit. This is the 'How'. Here are three steps you can take towards making this happen.

Successful strategies

- You can clarify your team's strategies for success
- You can flesh out your team's strategies for success
- You can implement your team's strategies for success

1) *You can clarify your team's strategies for success.*

You can clarify these key strategies either: a) by yourself; b) by involving a few senior managers; c) by involving the wider team. Imagine you have chosen the latter option. You are taking this route to give people a sense of ownership and also educate them about the bigger picture. As you are finally, responsible, however, it will ultimately be your decision on the ways forward.

The Strengths Toolbox

Gather the team together, communicate the picture of perfection and then invite people to tackle the exercise called *Successful strategies*. Bearing in mind the team's goals, invite them to brainstorm on the theme of:

The 3 key things we can do to give ourselves the greatest chance of success are:

*To ....

*To ....

*To ....

How to conduct the brainstorm? One approach is to give people 10 minutes to write their ideas on Post-It Notes – one idea per Post-It. Each person is then to go up in turn and post these ideas on a flip chart. They are to explain each idea and give concrete examples. Continue until everybody has finished. Move onto the next stage. Looking at the ideas, sort these into themes. If possible, go for 3 – or maximum 4 – themes. These will become your strategies for success. Discuss what has emerged and agree on your key strategies.

2) You can flesh out your team's strategies for success.

Now go into detail and flesh out the action plan. Invite interested parties – those who know the topics intimately – to focus on each of the three strategies. They must break these down into tactics and actions. Invite these work groups to present back their suggestions and, if all is agreed, you sign off the strategic plan. Communicate this plan to each team within the wider team. They must then present back how they will implement the strategies in their part of the business. Make sure you provide people with the support they need to implement the plan. So your plan may look something like this.

The 3 key things we can do to give ourselves the greatest chance of success are:

(1) To ....

    To ....

    To ....

    To ....

(2) To ....

    To ....

    To ....

    To ....

(3) To ....

    To ....

    To ....

    To ....

3) You can implement your team's strategies for success.

People can then get on with the work. Build in time every month for each team to report their successes; to share their action plans for the next month; to get help with tackling future challenges. Build in time every 3 months for 'course correction'. Double-check that people are on course and the strategies are still the most likely ones to achieve success. Be prepared to re-affirm or change them – but then keep people on track. Make sure that every business meeting agenda refers to the agreed strategies. You will then get people to focus and give themselves the greatest chance of success.

3 tips for building a team based on 'similarity of spirit' & 'diversity of strengths'

Super teams are made up of people who have similarity of spirit and diversity of strengths. Diversity of spirit is a recipe for disaster. So how can you build such a team? Let's explore these themes.

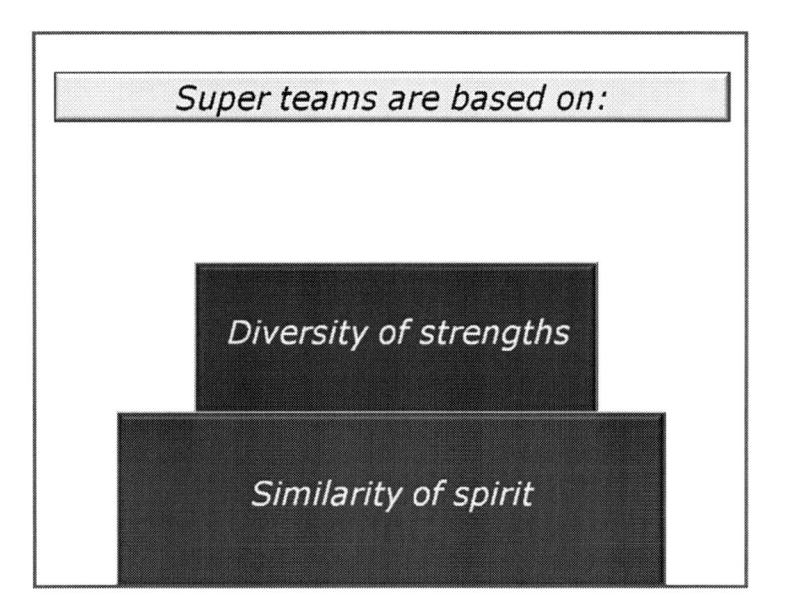

Super teams are based on:

Diversity of strengths

Similarity of spirit

1) *You can focus on similarity of spirit.*

Get the right people with the right attitude. Start by defining the spirit you want people in the team to demonstrate. Never compromise on spirit – otherwise you will pay a heavy price. One leader said:

"I want people: a) who take responsibility: b) who encourage other team members: c) who are customer focused. Once I hired a potentially brilliant person, but he behaved unprofessionally towards his colleagues. Despite giving him every opportunity to change his attitude, he continued to pursue his own agenda. It took months to repair the damage."

You may want to involve your team in defining the culture. If so, invite them to tackle the exercise described below. They are to describe the spirit – the attitude and behaviour – they want people in the team to demonstrate. Ask people to give concrete examples about how each quality would be translated into action.

Spirit

The spirit – attitude & behaviour – we want people in the team to demonstrate is:

*To ....

For example:..

*To ....

For example:..

*To ....

For example:..

Attitude is non-negotiable – but you want characters, not clones. People will express the team principles in many different ways – but it must always be within certain parameters. Recruit for spirit, then focus on the next step.

2) *You can focus on diversity of strengths.*

Spirit provides the foundation – but you will need creativity to achieve success. Virginia Satir, a pioneering family therapist, found that healthy families demonstrated two characteristics. First, they shared common values. Second, they encouraged people to be different within certain parameters. Sick families fought over their values and crushed differences. Great teams encourage people to use their

The Strengths Toolbox

talents. If you managed ABBA, you would encourage Agneta and Frida to sing, Bjorn and Benny to write the songs, not the other way round. If you led a start-up business, you would urge the brilliant sales person to get out on the road to find more customers, not spend 20 hours a week programming computers. Try tackling the following exercise.

Strengths

The strengths we already have in the team are people who have the ability:

*To ....

*To ....

*To ....

The strengths we need to add to the team are people who have the ability:

*To ....

*To ....

3) You can build a team with similarity of spirit and diversity of strengths.

Great teams get the right balance between consistency and creativity. Arnold Toynbee, the historian, believed this was also vital for societies that wished to survive. They must balance common ethics and creative endeavour. They needed imagination to respond to challenges that threatened their extinction. Looking back at the fall of societies, he wrote: "Civilizations die from suicide, not by murder...Civilizations in decline are constantly characterised by a tendency towards standardization and uniformity." Bearing this in mind, try completing the following sentence.

Super Teams

The specific things I can do to build a team with similarity of spirit and diversity of strengths are:

* ....
* ....
* ....

3 tips for getting the right balance of 'soul players' and 'star players'

Imagine you are a leader. You will need to make some tough decisions about the kinds of people you want in the team. Super teams get the right balance of 'soul players' and 'star players'. They have no room for 'semi-detached players'. Let's explore these themes.

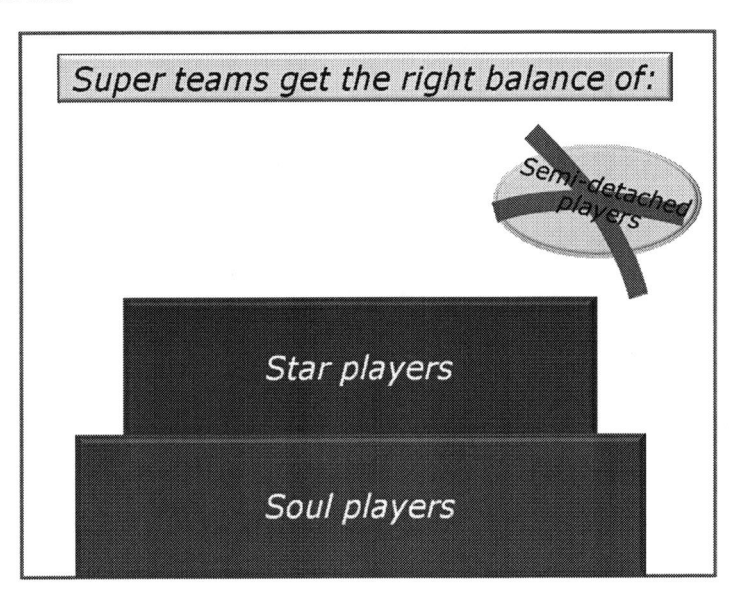

Super teams get the right balance of:

~~Semi-detached players~~

Star players

Soul players

1) You can get the right percentage of soul players.

Soul players embody the spirit of the team. They have a strong work ethic and do the right things every day. They provide the backbone and make sure the team always gets to at least 7/10. They are loyal and low-profile, but neglect them at your peril. Soul players need encouragement. They believe that, providing they do a good job, their loyalty will be rewarded. They may suffer in silence, however, while watching others grab attention. Reward them for their contribution – because otherwise one day you may find their resignation letter on your desk. "For years my partner kept telling me to move on because I wasn't appreciated," said one person. "It broke my heart to leave, but now it is time to think of myself." Good leaders make sure that around two-thirds of their team are soul players. Try completing the following sentences.

The soul players I already have in the team are:

* ....
* ....
* ....

The soul players I would like to add to the team are:

* ....

The specific things I can do to encourage the soul players are:

* ....

2) *You can get the right percentage of star players.*

Star players also embody the spirit – they work hard – but they add that 'touch of class'. They take the team from 7/10 to 10/10. Super teams often have around one-third of their team made up of star players. Talent brings obligations, however, so it is vital for such players to act as positive models. They must keep following the team principles and, when appropriate, add that touch of magic. Star players often act as 'Talismen' who can raise everybody's game.

How can you get the best out of such players? Contracting is crucial. Before you recruit – or 'rehire' – a potential star player it is vital to make sure that: a) They embody the team's spirit – otherwise it will be disastrous; b) They know the 'team's rules' before they commit to joining – or rejoining – otherwise they will make their own rules; c) They and you make clear contracts about their best contribution to the team. You can then work together to make magic. Try completing the following sentences.

The star players I already have in the team are:

* ....

* ....

* ....

The star players I would like to add to the team are:

* ....

The specific things I can do to encourage the star players are:

* ....

3) *You can move out the semi-detached players.*

Refuse to employ semi-detached players who show disregard for other people. They may well have exhausted previous managers who failed to 'motivate' them or find their talents. Everybody gets down at times but, if we choose to work for a team, this involves accepting a certain package. The deal includes: being professional, encouraging others and making our best contribution. Semi-detached players want to pursue their own agenda and often criticise other people.

"But what if I inherit a team which contains uncommitted people?" you may ask. *Before taking the job, make sure you have the mandate to build a super team.* You are then in a strong position when meeting each of the potentially difficult people. You are making the rules – not them. Meet with each person individually. Create an encouraging environment, but also give clear messages. Communicate the results, rules and rewards. Describe: a) The results the team is aiming to achieve; b) The 'rules' to be followed for achieving the results – the Dos and Don'ts; c) The rewards of reaching the goals. Then invite each person to go away, reflect and decide whether or not they want to opt into the team. *Remember, it is their job to persuade you they want to be in the team – not your job to persuade them.* People must actively make the decision to commit – or re-commit – to the team. They are then coming to work each day as volunteers, not as victims. If they do not commit – in actions, rather than words – they are choosing not to be in the team. Try completing the following sentences.

The semi-detached players I may have in the team are:

* ....

* ....

The steps I intend to take with them are:

* ....

Get the right balance of soul players and star players. You will then have the foundation for achieving future success.

3 tips for getting the right balance of decision-makers, drivers & deliverers

Imagine you are leading a team. Great teams get the right balance of decision makers, drivers and deliverers. Decision-makers set the strategy. Drivers act as the gears – they 'live the message' and translate the ideas into action. Deliverers produce the goods. People may move between all three roles at times but, by and large, it is important to get the right balance in your team. Let's explore what this means in practice.

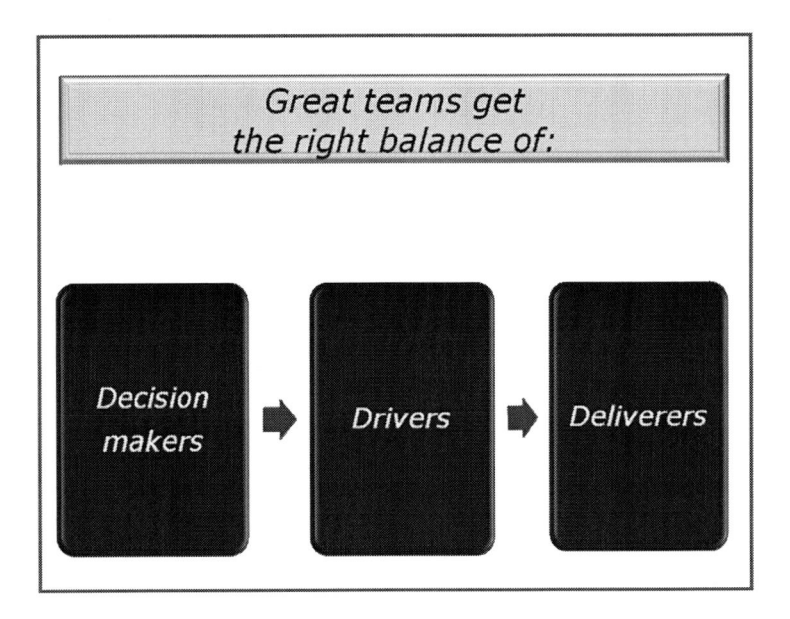

Great teams get the right balance of:

Decision makers ➡ **Drivers** ➡ **Deliverers**

1) Decision-makers.

Decision-makers set the compass. They clarify what mountain the team are climbing, why they are climbing it and when they will reach the summit. They communicate this story in a compelling way and ensure everybody knows their part in achieving the goals. Great teams frequently have two or three people at the centre who take responsibility for setting the overall direction. Depending on the topics to be covered, however, they then involve wider groups. Leaders do this to ensure people have a real sense of ownership regarding their part of their strategy. How does this work in your team? Try completing the following sentences.

The good decision-makers we already have in the team are:

* ....

* ....

* ....

The decision-makers we may need to add to the team are:

* ....

2) Drivers.

Drivers are the gears of the team. They act as positive models and often lead 'teams within the team'. They approach the leaders and say: "As far as I understand it, the strategy is … My part and my team's part in making the strategy happen is … Is that correct? Right, I will go and make it happen." Leaders must make sure that *all* their direct reports embody these qualities. Otherwise they will leapfrog them and micro-manage the deliverers. Great football clubs, for example, recruit drivers to form spine of the team. Spurring on their team mates, they ensure the strategy is translated into action. How does this work in your team? Try completing the following sentence.

The good drivers we already have in the team are:

* ....

* ....

* ....

The Strengths Toolbox

The drivers we may need to add to the team are:

* ....

3) *Deliverers.*

Deliverers are often experts and do great work. Some deliverers do go on to become drivers – but that calls for them taking a different kind of responsibility. They must be prepared to act as positive models and make tough decisions. Some deliverers therefore prefer to remain brilliant niche providers. This is okay: providing they have a positive attitude, do good work and contribute to helping the team reach its goals. How does this work in your team? Try completing the following sentence.

The good deliverers we already have in the team are:

* ....

* ....

* ....

The deliverers we may need to add to the team are:

* ....

Super teams get the right balance of decision makers, drivers and deliverers. So, if you wish, tackle the exercise at the end of this piece that brings everything together. Clarify what you can do to get the right people in the right places. This will give your team the greatest chance of success.

Decision-makers, drivers & deliverers. Action plan

The specific things we must therefore do to get the right people in the right places in the team are:

* ....

Super Teams

* ....
* ....

3 tips for making a clear contract with your team

Imagine you are a team leader. One of your first jobs will be to make a clear working contract with the team. People must be clear on: a) The leader's responsibilities; b) The team members' responsibilities. The contract should cover both the psychological and practical responsibilities of working together. Here is one approach you can take to making such an agreement. Gather the team and invite them to focus on the following themes.

The super teams contract	
The leader's responsibility is:	The team members' responsibility is:
* To	* To
* To	* To
* To	* To
* To	* To
* To	* To

1) You can clarify the leader's responsibility in the team.

Invite people to brainstorm what they see as the leader's role in ensuring the team reaches its goals. For example, to provide a clear vision; to manage upwards and provide 'air cover' – protecting them from interference; to create an encouraging environment; to give people practical support; to make clear contracts about each person's contribution; to co-ordinate everybody's strengths; to make tough decisions; to do what is necessary to guide the team to success.

The leader's responsibility is:

* ....
* ....
* ....
* ....
* ....

There will be a chance to discuss these ideas later – but first move onto the next stage.

2) You can clarify the team members' responsibility in the team.

Invite people to brainstorm what they see as the team members' role in ensuring the team reaches its goals. For example, to choose to be in the team; to have a positive attitude; to understand the team's vision; to make clear contracts about their best contribution; to encourage their colleagues; to be creative; to come with solutions, rather than problems; to deliver on their promises; to do whatever is necessary to help the team to achieve success.

The team members' responsibility is:

* ....
* ....
* ....
* ....
* ....

The Strengths Toolbox

Again, there will be a chance to discuss these ideas later – but then move onto the next stage.

3) You can clarify and agree on the team's working contract.

Looking at the ideas under the respective responsibilities, invite people to arrange these under themes and discuss the topics. When you feel people are ready, invite the team members to agree to the team's working contract. As the leader, you will have the final say, but team members often produce an excellent agreement. Conclude by writing up the contract and, if appropriate, putting it in a place where people can see it each day.

How can you use the contract? There are two main ways. First, it provides a constant reminder of people's respective responsibilities. Second, it can be used when tackling difficult situations. For example, if a person behaves badly, don't get dragged down into arguing about the details. Just go back to the contract. Ask whether they want to follow or change the contract. Sometimes it may be appropriate to alter the conditions – but then make sure the whole team are in agreement. If a person continues to break the rules, however, they are choosing to leave the team. Clear contracting provides the basis for building a successful team.

3 tips for knowing when to 'debate, decide, deliver'

Imagine you are leading a team. The 'debate, decide, deliver' model is a good one for involving your people in owning parts of the strategy. Let's look at how this works in practice. Start by giving people clear guidelines about the freedom they have to operate with the 3 Ds.

- Debate: describe the topics that are not up for debate – because these have already been decided – and those that are.

- Decide: describe the parameters within which people can then make decisions.

- Deliver: describe the deadlines by which people will be expected to deliver.

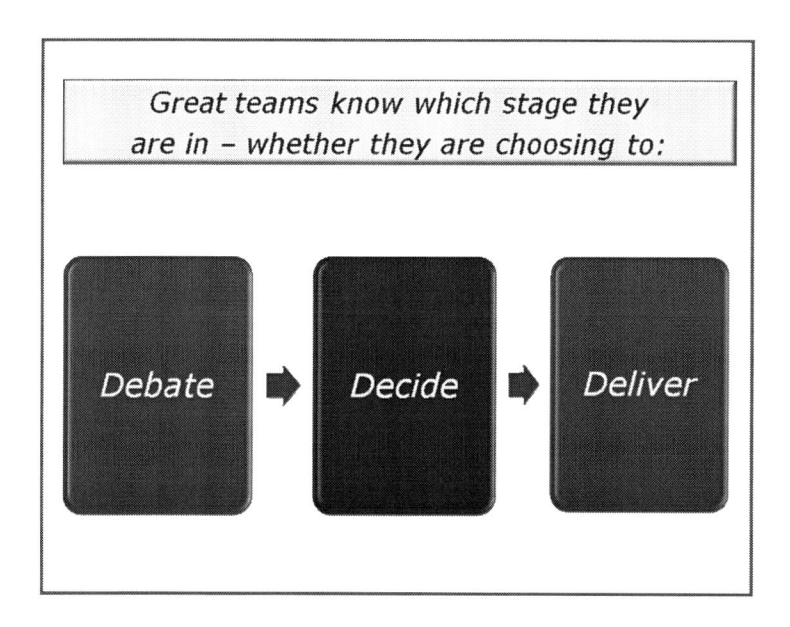

Great teams know which stage they are in – whether they are choosing to:

Debate ➡ **Decide** ➡ **Deliver**

Great teams know which part of the model they are operating in. They know whether they are debating, deciding or delivering. Poor teams get the three parts mixed up. Bearing these principles in mind, let's consider how you can guide your team through the three steps.

1) Debate.

Describe again the areas that people can and can't debate. You may say, for example:

"The big 'What' – the result we must deliver – is not open to debate. The key strategies – the 'How' – have also been handed down. What we can discuss, however, are the tactics within each of these strategies.

Here are the topics that we can debate as a team.

a)..

b)..

c)..

"Are there any other topics to add that perhaps fall under our remit to discuss? Let's add those to the list. Right, let's explore the first topic."

Embark on the debate process. Clarity is crucial. Looking at the first topic, start by defining the results to deliver. Move onto the choices and consequences. Brainstorm all the possible options – together with the pluses and minuses of each option. Discuss the options, then move onto finding possible creative solutions. Eventually you will find the group start moving towards their conclusions.

Good facilitation will be required. Get the right balance between 'opening up' – clarifying the result to achieve and exploring ideas – then 'closing down'. Create an atmosphere in which people share their ideas. Business meetings sometimes close down the discussion too early. On the other hand, some teams open up subject after subject and never make any decisions. Get the right balance when discussing the first topic. Then, when appropriate, move onto the next stage.

2) *Decide.*

Time to make a decision. You may say something like: "Looking at the first topic, let's return to results to deliver. Now is the time to decide on which option – or options – we want to pursue. After making the decision, we must then decide who will do what by when. Okay, looking at the first topic, let's decide on the route forward."

Clarify the action plan for the first topic. Continue the session by repeating the 'Debate' and 'Decide' steps for other items on the agenda. Conclude the session by summarising what has been agreed. Encourage people to 'play back' what they understand to be the action plans for delivering the team's goals. Then move onto the next stage.

3) *Deliver.*

People must then work hard to deliver. Provide the support they need to do the job. Super teams are made up of people who are positive, professional and peak performers. But sometimes they get thrown off course. If people become paralysed in long discussions, investigate the reasons. If appropriate, return to the 'debate, decide and deliver' model. Check that the 'debate' and 'decide' parts have been agreed. If so – and if the decision still fits – then ensure they deliver. If not, then ensure people make a decision and deliver. (Sometimes, of course, it can be a case of 'just do it'.)

Let's return to your own team. Try completing the following exercise on the 3 Ds.

The Strengths Toolbox

Debate

The specific things I can do to make clear to people what they can and can't debate are:

* ....
* ....
* ....

Decide

The specific things I can do to enable people to make good decisions within these parameters are:

* ....
* ....
* ....

Deliver

The specific things I can do to ensure that people then know when they must deliver are:

* ....
* ....
* ....

Super teams have crystal clear goals. People know what mountain they are climbing, why they are climbing it and when they will reach the summit. Within this framework, people work best when they can 'own' their part of the strategy. Providing it is used properly, the 3 D model is a good tool for making this happen. People then develop the habit of knowing when to debate, decide and deliver.

3 tips for clarifying each person's contribution to the picture of perfection

Imagine you are a team leader. Let's assume that you have finalised the team's goals following the principles outlined in the piece called 3 tips for clarifying the team's picture of perfection. Here are three steps you can take towards encouraging each person to make their best contribution towards achieving the goals.

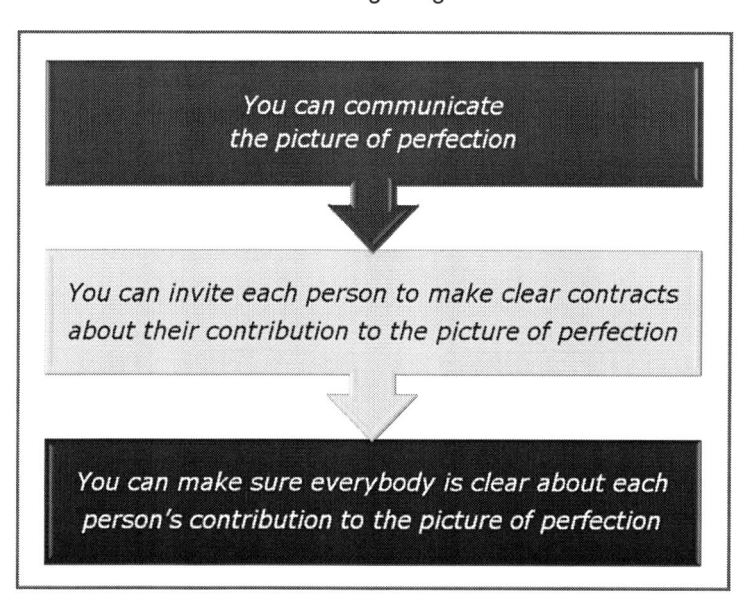

You can communicate the picture of perfection

⬇

You can invite each person to make clear contracts about their contribution to the picture of perfection

⬇

You can make sure everybody is clear about each person's contribution to the picture of perfection

1) *You can communicate the picture of perfection.*

Start by communicating the picture of perfection. Make sure that everybody is clear on 'What' the team is aiming to achieve; 'Why' it is aiming to achieve it – the benefits; 'How' it is aiming to achieve it – the key strategies; 'Who' should be doing what; 'When' things will be happening on the journey. Make sure people are clear on the road map – then move onto the next stage.

2) You can invite each person to clarify and make clear contracts about their contribution to the picture of perfection.

Give everybody the chance to describe the part they would like to play by completing the exercise *My contribution to the picture of perfection*. Give them 60 minutes to clarify their best contribution. They are to describe: a) The goals they want to deliver; b) The benefits of achieving these goals – how it will contribute to the POP; c) The style in which they work best; d) The support they would like to do the job. e) The measures – the specific things that will be happening that will show they have reached the goals. Meet with each person to finalise their contribution and make clear contracts about their part in achieve the picture of perfection. Then move onto the final part.

My contribution to the picture of perfection

The goals. *The specific results I aim to deliver are:*

* ....
* ....
* ....

The benefits. *The contribution this will make to achieving the picture of perfection is:*

* ....
* ....
* ....

The style. *The way I work best is:*

* ....
* ....
* ....

The support. *The support I would like is:*

* ....
* ....
* ....

The measures. *The specific things that will show I have reached the goals will be:*

* ....
* ....
* ....

3) You can gather the team and make sure everybody is clear on each person's part in achieving the picture of perfection.

Gather the team together. Invite each person to make a 10 minutes presentation to the whole team about their contribution. Everybody then knows what mountain they are climbing, why they are climbing it and everybody's part in reaching the summit.

This model works – providing people keep returning to the POP. Great teams do not look for some new 'magic bullet'. They keep focusing on the goal. For example, they make it the compass for every meeting. People must show how what they are going to discuss relates to achieving the POP. You can also build in monthly meetings for 'course correction' – making sure they are on track. Invite people to present: a) The things they have done in the past month towards achieving the POP; b) The things they intend to do in the next month; c) The potential challenges they face; d) The support they need to reach the goals. Keep people on track until they deliver the picture of perfection.

3 tips for co-ordinating your team's strengths

Imagine you are leader and want to co-ordinate your team's talents to achieve concrete results. There are two main approaches you can take: the 'conventional' way and the 'creative' way. Here are some ideas to consider.

1) You can follow the 'conventional' way.

This is the 'organisational' approach used by many older style teams. a) They define the results to be achieved – the 'What'. b) They define the roles to be filled and draw an organisational chart with the appropriate boxes. c) They fill these boxes with job descriptions, skills and competencies. d) They interview people and try to match them to the boxes. e) They start working.

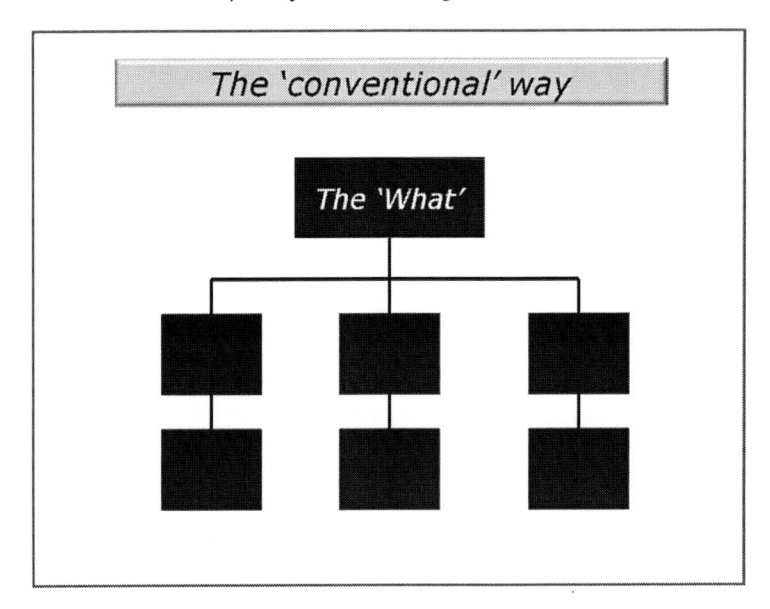

The 'conventional' way

The 'What'

The pluses are: It looks orderly; it will often get you to 7/10. The minuses are: People must fit themselves into the boxes; they may only use their strengths to 70%; time is spent chasing up people about gaps in performance; it will seldom get you to 10/10. Let's explore another approach.

2) You can follow the 'creative' way.

This is the 'organic' approach used by many super teams. a) They define the results to be achieved – the 'What'. b) Looking at available people, they ask: "What are their 'A' talents? How can we co-ordinate these strengths to reach the goal?" c) They ask: "What are the gaps? How can we fill these?" d) They make clear contracts about each person's contribution to the team. e) They co-ordinate people's talents to reach the goal.

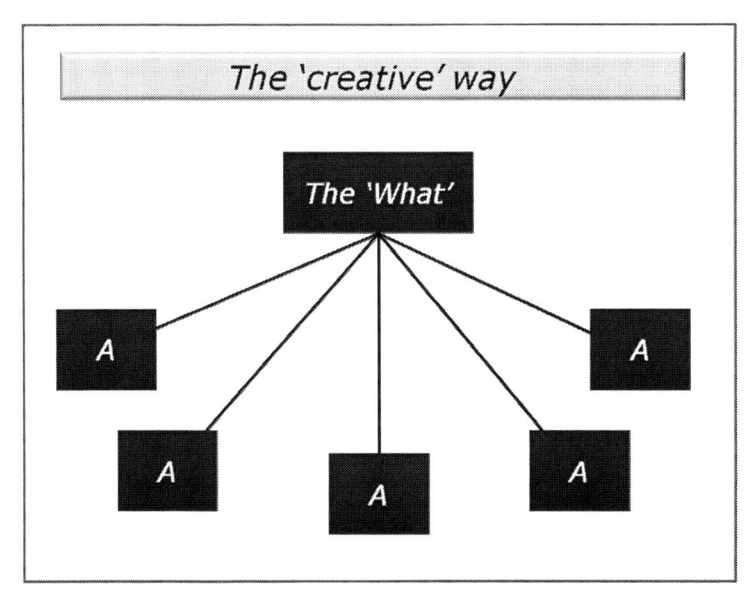

The 'creative' way

The 'What'

A   A   A   A   A

The pluses are: People play to their strengths and feel fulfilled; the gaps get filled; the team goes from good to great – scoring between 9/10 – 10/10. The minuses: Calls for super team work based on clarity, contracting and concrete results; needs time to

The Strengths Toolbox

keep asking: "How can we fill the gaps?"; sometimes this requires unconventional answers; the team needs a co-ordinator.

3) You can sometimes combine both the 'conventional' and 'creative' ways to reach your goals.

"Can I combine both methods?" somebody may ask. Some leaders do. They start by drawing a conventional organisational chart, give it a go and may reach 7/10. Taking a reality check, they ask: "What is and isn't working? How can we build on the best and find solutions to the rest?" Recalling their original template, they realise there is seldom a 'perfect fit' between it and the people. So they move onto the creative approach. They get people to play to their strengths, whilst finding solutions to the other challenges.

You will, of course, follow this path in your own way. Try completing the following sentence.

The specific things I can do to co-ordinate people's strengths in my team are:

* ....

* ....

* ....

Super teams have a crystal clear goal. They have the right people implementing the right strategy in the right way. They put round pegs in round holes. The conventional approach can produce work that is good – but the creative approach will deliver work that is great.

3 tips for communicating your leadership style to people

Good leaders communicate how they will behave as leaders. Why? Team members like to know what to expect, otherwise they can spend months trying to figure out the 'rules. Let's explore three steps you can take to communicate your leadership style to people.

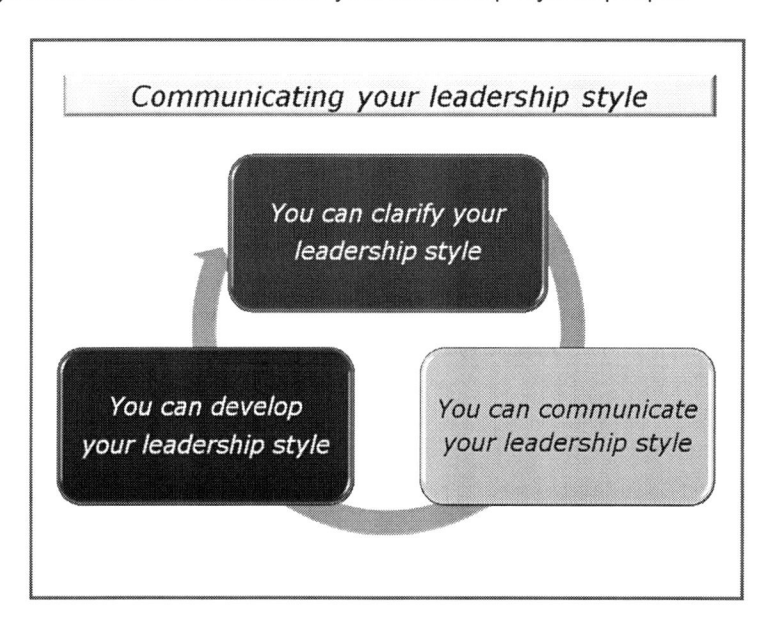

1) You can clarify your leadership style.

Try tackling the exercise on this theme called *My leadership style*. This invites you to describe your operating style under four main headings.

- **The way I will work as a leader.**

Describe what you will and won't do as a leader. Be honest and realistic. *Don't make this a wish list.* Simply describe how you will behave and be as specific as possible. One person wrote:

The Strengths Toolbox

I will:
- Be full of energy in a morning, possibly ringing you before 8.00.
- Get to the point quickly in conversations, rather than do lots of social chat.
- Provide a clear vision for the team, but give you freedom, within limits, on how you get to the goal.
- Talk quickly, but sometimes not check out that you have understood what I have said.
- Often use sporting analogies.
- Protect you from unnecessary interference from my bosses – but expect you to deliver on your promises.
- Expect you to take responsibility.
- Etc.

I won't:
- Always look at you directly when you are speaking. I will look at you when we start the conversation, but then may look away when trying to make sense of the information. Please do not take this personally. I really am listening.
- Be good at giving praise. I set the bar high for myself and other people. The times I do give praise are when somebody performs exceptionally.
- Get involved in lots of social events. For example, I will also go to bed early on off-sites, rather than sit around talking into the early hours.
- Etc.

- **The best way to work with me.**

Describe the 'Dos' and 'Don'ts' for working with you as the leader. One person wrote:

Do:
- Be professional. For example, be on time for meetings; encourage your colleagues; always think of things from the customer's point of view.

* Prepare properly for one-to-one sessions with me. At the start of the session explain what you want to discuss and what you want from me.
* Manage your own career development, though I will provide the resources and support.
* Be honest. For example, let me know bad news quickly. It's good if you can outline the possible options for moving forward, but don't hide bad news if you have not yet thought of a strategy.
* Be contactable. I won't track where you are – you may be dropping your child off for school – but make sure you are reachable between 8.00 and 18.00.
* Do keep your promises – do what you say you are going to do.
* Accept that we work for an American company. This won't always be easy, but we are all adults and have chosen to work for the company.
* Etc.

Don't:
* Come unprepared to meetings.
* Put your own agenda before that of the team.
* Waffle.
* Etc.

- **The consequences of my style.**

Describe what you see as the pluses and minuses of your style. This will show people you are aware there are both upsides and downsides to the way you operate – both for yourself and other people.

- **The specific things I can to do build on the pluses and minimise the minuses.**

Describe how you can build on your strengths and manage the consequences of your weaknesses. Consider which parts of your style you want to develop and which to moderate; simply because doing this will produce better results.

2) *You can communicate your leadership style to people in your team.*

Find an appropriate time to share your leadership style with your team. I have often invited leaders to do this during a super team workshop – but other times can also be appropriate. Providing it is communicated properly, the response is normally positive. People like to know how you operate, so it's good to make the implicit explicit. They can then take a stand towards how they work with you. A typical reaction came from one team member who told their leader:

"We have been working together for 5 years, but this document sums you up, warts and all. For example, it took me 6 months to figure out that you have a memory like an elephant, even though you seldom write anything down. At first I thought you weren't paying attention during our conversations, but later you could recount every detail. Now I tell new starters to ignore your body language, which can be a bit disconcerting. They need to know that you notice every detail about them and the conversation. Some people find this intimidating, but most eventually get used to you. I wish somebody had told me your 'rules' when I first joined the team."

As mentioned earlier, here is the framework for the exercise.

My leadership style

I will:

* ....

* ....

* ....

I won't:

* ....

* ....

* ....

The best way to work with me

Do:

* ……………………………………………………………………
* ……………………………………………………………………
* ……………………………………………………………………

Don't:

* ……………………………………………………………………
* ……………………………………………………………………
* ……………………………………………………………………

The consequences of my style

Pluses:

* ……………………………………………………………………
* ……………………………………………………………………
* ……………………………………………………………………

Minuses:

* ……………………………………………………………………
* ……………………………………………………………………
* ……………………………………………………………………

The specific things I can do to build on the pluses and minimise the minuses are:

* ……………………………………………………………………
* ……………………………………………………………………
* ……………………………………………………………………

3) You can develop your leadership style.

One leader explained: "The pluses of my style are that: a) Because I am so focused, it is likely that we will reach our goals: b) Self-managing people will thrive: c) Everybody will learn. The possible minuses are that: a) Sometimes I will fail to give positive strokes, even though I know I should: b) Not everybody finds it easy to work with me."

"Building on the pluses, I will continue to provide direction and give people the tools they need to do their jobs. Aiming to minimise the minuses, I will spend one hour with each person every two months. Ahead of the meeting, please send me an email describing: a) The specific things you have done well during the two months: b) The things you think you can do better in the future – and how: c) The plans you have for the next two months and the practical support you need from me."

Team members often appreciate the honesty you put into the exercise. Remember: there are no 'good' or 'bad' styles – there are just consequences!

3 tips for communicating the results, rules and rewards

Imagine you are a leader. You are gathering the team to focus on the road ahead. People are motivated and enjoy being in the team. They are volunteers, not victims. They have already done a lot of work on clarifying the picture of perfection. People have also made clear contracts about their individual contributions towards achieving the goals. Here are three themes you can cover when communicating with your team. The messages may appear blunt – but they will enable people to refocus before 'entering the arena'.

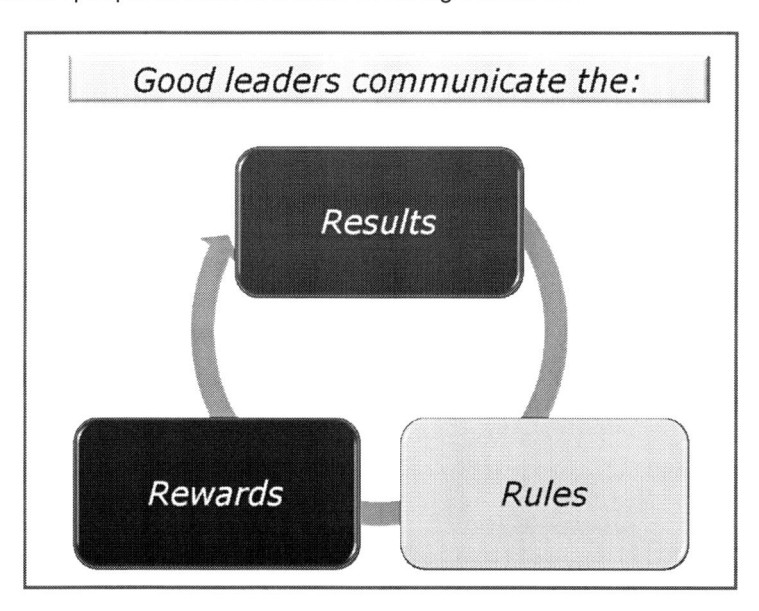

Good leaders communicate the:

- Results
- Rules
- Rewards

1) *You can communicate the results.*

Describe the results the team are aiming to achieve – this is the 'What'. You can also give the reasons – the 'Why'. Great orators provide the call to action by painting pictures of the goal. They say things like: "We are going to put a man on the moon by the end of the decade...We are going to do it – not because it is easy, but because it is hard." Good leaders are authentic, however, so it is vital to be yourself. Paint these pictures in your own way. Try completing the following sentence.

The things I can do to communicate the results are:

* ....
* ....
* ....

2) *You can communicate the rules.*

Describe the 'rules' that people must follow to deliver the results – this is the 'How'. For example: "These are the Dos and Don'ts for reaching the goals. Do take responsibility, make clear contracts, be customer focused and deliver the goods. Never walk past a quality problem." Every team has rules – spoken or unspoken – so bring these out into the open. Explain the reasons for following the rules. Do two things once you have outlined these guidelines: a) reward the behaviour you want repeated; b) never ignore it if somebody breaks the rules.

One key point. You are saying that 'these are the rules around here'. You are not saying these are right or wrong – just that these are the rules for tackling this particular project. For example, a football manager may say: "I do not play players who smoke." One player may say: "So are you saying that we must not smoke?" The manager will reply: "No, you can smoke if you want – but you won't play for the team again. It is your choice."

Bearing in mind the 'project' you want to tackle, try completing the following sentence.

The things I can do to communicate the rules are:

* ....
* ....
* ....

3) *You can communicate the rewards.*

Describe the pluses of reaching the goals – for the company, the customers and the colleagues. Dare to outline the possible minuses. You want responsible people who choose to opt in—so be straight. Ernest Shackleton took this approach when advertising in *The Times* for people to accompany him to the South Pole. He declared there would be: "no pay, terrible conditions and little likelihood of return." He received hundreds of applications. Try completing the following sentence.

The things I can do to communicate the rewards are:

* ....
* ....
* ....

Good leaders communicate the results, rules and rewards. You can describe these to show the road ahead – but sometimes you can do so much earlier, such as when people apply to join the team. They then know what they are signing up for. People also know the guidelines they can follow to help the team to achieve success.

3 tips for balancing being an energiser, educator and enforcer

Imagine you are a leader. You will develop your own leadership style, but there are also some useful models that you can apply in your own way. Great leaders, for example, often combine the elements of being an energiser, educator and enforcer. Let's explore these areas.

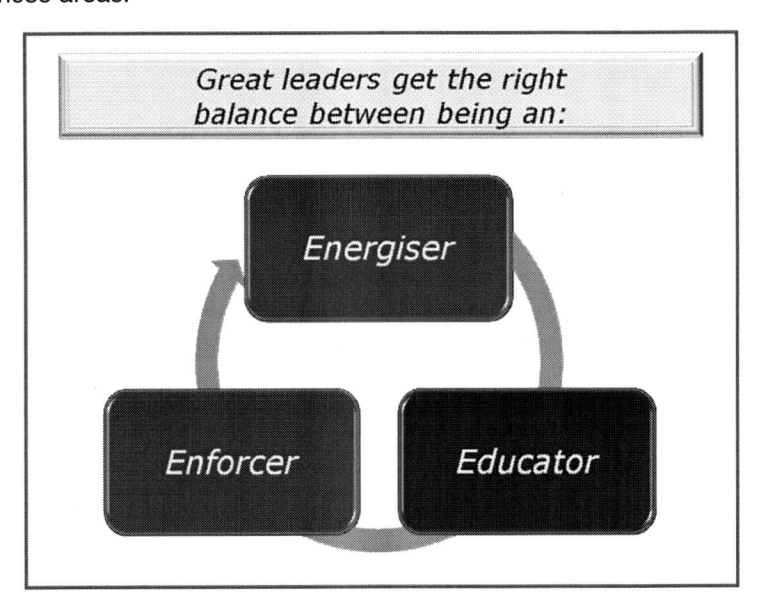

Great leaders get the right balance between being an:

- Energiser
- Enforcer
- Educator

1) You can be an energiser.

Good leaders provide an inspiring vision. They communicate a clear strategy and show people the road towards achieving the picture of perfection. Team members must be self-motivated – but they can also be lifted by a leader who is energetic and enthusiastic. How would you rate yourself as an energiser for your team? Do this on a scale 0 – 10. Then describe what you can do to maintain or improve the rating.

Energiser

The rating I would give myself as an energiser for my team is: ____ /10

The specific things I can do to maintain or improve the rating are:

* ....
* ....
* ....

2) *You can be an educator.*

Good leaders provide an encouraging environment in which people can develop. Team members are then more able to execute the strategy and achieve the picture of perfection. You can pass on your knowledge in many different ways. When appropriate, for example, explain your decision-making process. Outline the challenges, choices, consequences, creative solutions and conclusions. People will then be more equipped to make decisions in their daily work. This releases you as a leader to shape tomorrow's business, rather than get stuck in managing today's business. How do you rate yourself as an educator for your team? Do this on a scale 0 – 10. Then describe what you can do to maintain or improve the rating.

Educator

The rating I would give myself as an educator for my team is: ....____ /10

The specific things I can do to maintain or improve the rating are:

* ....
* ....
* ....

The Strengths Toolbox

3) You can be an enforcer.

Good leaders provide the compass – the code of conduct – for the team. They are also prepared to enforce the Dos and Don'ts for achieving the picture of perfection. The leader must set the tone and, if necessary, make tough decisions about conduct – but the team members must also take responsibility. Part of the 'education' process is providing a moral framework that everybody understands. People must see how following certain guidelines will help them to achieve success. It is then up to individuals to decide whether or not they want to opt into the team. Great teams are characterised by team members who are prepared to 'enforce' the agreed standards with each other. Old style leaders sometimes relied on autocratic enforcement without providing education. They ended up chasing their own tails, complaining about the quality of staff. How would you rate yourself as an enforcer for your team? Do this on a scale 0 – 10. Then describe what you can do to maintain or improve the rating.

Enforcer

The rating I would give myself as an enforcer for my team is: ____ /10

The specific things I can do to maintain or improve the rating are:

* ....

* ....

* ....

Energy provides inspiration, but education enables people to achieve excellence. Enforcement is crucial to provide the compass and credo. Great leaders combine all three elements to increase the chances of success.

3 tips for following the STAGE model of leadership

Great leaders often follow the STAGE Model of leadership. This covers the Strategic, Tactical, Administrative, Grunt work and Emotional aspects of teamwork. They personally often focus on the strategic and emotional leadership – whilst hiring people who manage the TAG part. Imagine you are a leader. Here are three suggestions to bear in mind when following the STAGE model.

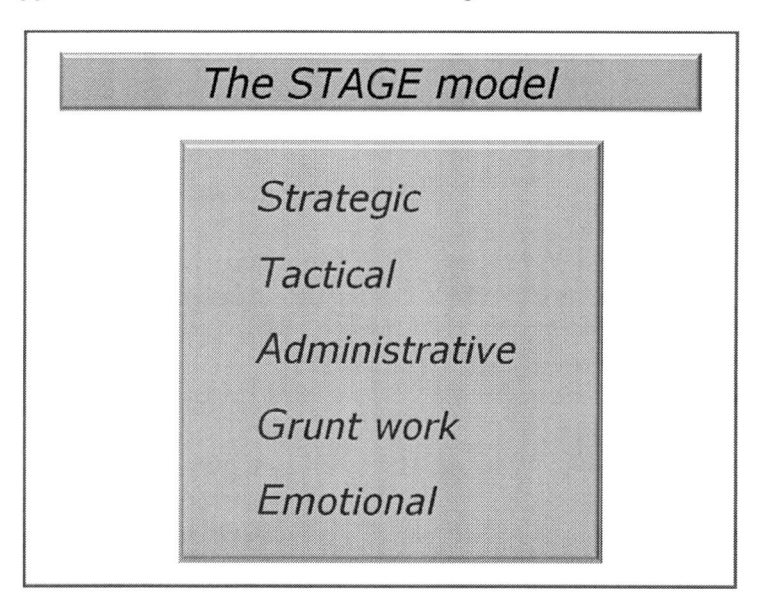

```
The STAGE model

    Strategic

    Tactical

    Administrative

    Grunt work

    Emotional
```

1) You can provide the strategic leadership

Great leaders communicate the strategy for achieving success. Your job is to keep people's eyes on the picture of perfection. Keep communicating: a) The 'What' – the goal we are aiming to achieve; b) The 'Why' – the reasons we are doing it and the benefits; c) The 'How' – the strategy for achieving the goal; d) The 'Who' – the people who are doing what to achieve the goal; e) The 'When' – the milestones along the way – plus when we will know that we have reached the goals. Keep communicating the big picture, especially when it gets tough. People need to keep their eyes on the longer term picture of success. Try completing the following sentence – then move onto the implementation part.

The specific things I can do to provide strategic leadership are:

* ....

* ....

* ....

2) You can make sure the tactics, administration and grunt work get done.

Great leaders may have grand strategies – but these must be translated into action. As a leader, you can try to do everything yourself, but you will then be doomed to failure. Your job is to focus on the strategic and emotional leadership. If appropriate, get a co-ordinator to oversee the TAG part, otherwise you will fall into fire-fighting. Their job is to oversee three things.

- **Tactics** – to ensure that grand plans are translated into tactics that contribute to achieving the goals.
- **Administration** – to ensure that diaries are kept up to date, meetings scheduled and the hygiene factors managed, otherwise the team falls into chaos.
- **Grunt Work** – to ensure people are encouraged, equipped and enabled to do the daily tasks – and that these are completed.

The co-ordinator may not actually do all the work themselves – but they do ensure it gets done. "Must it be one person?" somebody may ask. "I have four people reporting into me. Can't they all act as co-ordinators?" Yes, they can, but as soon as it gets beyond four reports, the leader may find themselves turning into a manager, rather than a leader. Every great team I have met has had a superb co-ordinator. Try completing the following sentence – then move onto the final step.

The specific things I can do to make sure the tactical, administrative and grunt work parts get done are:

* ....
* ....
* ....

3) *You can provide emotional leadership.*

Great leaders harness people's emotional energy to achieve the goals. Different leaders do this in different ways. Some are good in 'one-to-many' situations. They give inspiring speeches and provide rallying calls to action. Some are good in 'one-to-few' situations. They prefer small groups where they can listen, connect with people's agendas and find positive solutions. Some are good in 'one-to-one' situations. They provide the personal touch, make individuals feel valued and encourage them to do their best work.

Great leaders play to their strengths – and few are good in all situations. Some are good as strategic leaders, for example, but fail to provide the necessary emotional leadership. They often work best in tandem with somebody who can connect with people emotionally. Bearing in mind your strengths, try completing the following sentence.

The specific things I can do to provide emotional leadership are:

* ....
* ....
* ....

The Strengths Toolbox

There are many models of leadership. The STAGE model is just one. The key is the emotional part. Great leaders inspire people to put their hearts – as well as their heads – into reaching the goal.

3 tips for being a good co-ordinator

Great teams always have a co-ordinator. Why? Getting creative people to combine their talents can be challenging at the best of times. The co-ordinator's role is to ensure people channel their talents towards achieving the team's goal. Let's see how this works in practice.

Clarity is vital. The leader's role is to chart the way towards achieving the picture of perfection. The team member's job is to clarify their best contribution and commit to achieving the goals. They must then do creative work, co-operate and achieve concrete results. Sounds simple in theory – but things can go wrong, especially during the creative work stage. Strong orchestration is vital – otherwise individuals may do their own thing.

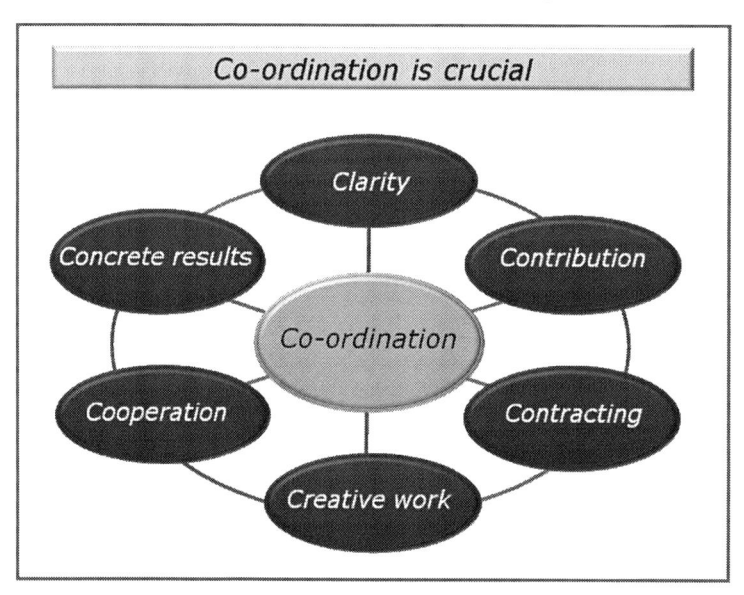

Co-ordination is crucial

- Clarity
- Contribution
- Contracting
- Creative work
- Cooperation
- Concrete results
- Co-ordination

"But isn't that the leader's job?" somebody may ask. As was mentioned in the last piece, great leaders often follow the STAGE Model of leadership. They focus on the strategic and emotional leadership – whilst hiring the right people to manage the tactics,

The Strengths Toolbox

administration and grunt work. Great leaders have a co-ordinator who makes this happen – otherwise they get sucked down into fire-fighting. Let's explore three of the key steps in being a good co-ordinator.

1) You can establish clarity.

Clarity is crucial if you are going to play the role successfully. Start by clarifying: a) The leader's specific goals – the picture of perfection; b) The strategy for achieving the goals; c) The leader's role in reaching the goals and the role they want you to play as the co-ordinator. Clarify the Dos & Don'ts involved in your role. Good leaders communicate your role to the team. People then know your areas of accountability, autonomy and authority.

Credibility is also crucial – especially in the eyes of the team members. Good co-ordinators gain respect by: a) Showing they respect the team members and their knowledge; b) Showing they want to support people, rather than becoming a hindrance; c) Showing some early successes – such as getting resources, removing obstacles or producing quick visible results.

2) You can do the co-ordination.

Good co-ordinators ask questions such as: "What are the results we want to achieve – the picture of perfection? What are the resources available? What is each person's 'A' talent? How can we co-ordinate these talents to achieve the goal? What support will they need to achieve success? How can I provide this support? What are the Dos and Don'ts with each person? How can I make clear contracts with them about their contribution towards achieving the goal?"

Good co-ordinators then make things happen. They are like sheepdogs, especially with knowledge workers who may fall into following their own agendas. Approaching such a person, they say things like: "Tell me how things are going……That is interesting. Now, remember the agreed picture of perfection. Is that something you still want to contribute towards achieving? If so, can you get back to me as to how you would like to continue contributing towards achieving the goals? Then I will provide the support you need. Great if you can get back to me within the next day." Like sheepdogs, they are friendly, but sometimes bare their teeth. They get away with it because the team members respect them – and also know they can be tough.

3) You can deliver concrete results.

Good co-ordinators get some early wins, rather than embark on long process analyses. Success breeds success. It also buys time to tackle the more long-standing challenges. Good co-ordinators see their role as proactive – rather than that of a glorified progress-chaser. So build in weekly meetings with the leader to look ahead to the next week, the month, the next quarter. Clarify the challenges facing the team and agree on the potential solutions. Some team members may try to split you – like a child approaching different parents till they get the 'right answer'. The co-ordinator may also need to 'manage' the leader – to ensure that person makes their best contribution to the business.

"When it was first mentioned to me, I did not understand the role of the co-ordinator," said one leader. "Looking back at my earlier career, however, I realised my best work had been when I had someone who made things happen. They are now the first person I look for when taking over a new team. A good co-ordinator is worth their weight in gold."

Try tackling the exercise on this theme. Imagine a situation where you want to act as a good co-ordinator. Try completing the following sentences.

Clarity

The things I can do to establish clarity are:

* ....
* ....
* ....

The Strengths Toolbox

Co-ordination

The things I can do to provide good co-ordination are:

* ....
* ....
* ....

Concrete results

The things I can do to deliver concrete results are:

* ....
* ....
* ....

Great leaders and co-ordinators get their act together. They know that clarity is the starting point for any venture. But co-ordination is the bridge to producing concrete results.

3 tips for balancing consistency and creativity in a team

Imagine you are a leader. Great teams consistently reach 8/10 – but they also encourage people to express their talents so the team reaches 10/10. You want to build such a team – but you may be concerned that people sometimes neglect the basics on their route to self-expression. Here are three tips for getting the right combination in your team.

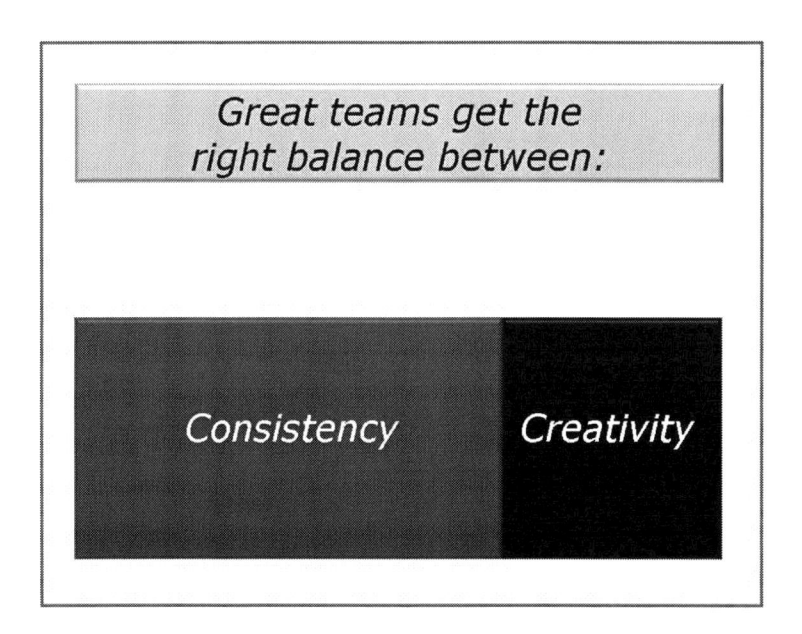

> **Great teams get the right balance between:**
>
> *Consistency*   *Creativity*

1) *You can encourage people to do certain things consistently.*

Gather people together. Start by explaining how superb teams get the right balance between consistency and creativity. Then invite them to tackle the exercise on this theme. People are to start by agreeing on the things that everybody must do in a consistent way.

The Strengths Toolbox

For example, during the 80s I had the opportunity to work with teams of talented young footballers. The remit was to encourage the players to think for themselves, rather than continually look to the bench. When tackling this exercise with one football team, they agreed that everybody should:

"Arrive on time for training; keep themselves fit; listen to the coach; follow the team game plan; stick to their agreed roles during matches; always give 100%; accept the referee's decisions without dissent; encourage each other in adversity; always take responsibility – do not blame other people."

So invite people to brainstorm and then agree on the following things.

Consistency

The things people must do in a consistent way are:

* ....

* ....

* ....

2) You can encourage people to also use their creativity.

Move onto the second part. Ask people to brainstorm and agree on when it important to encourage individuals to use their creativity. After some discussion, the football team agreed that players should use their imagination when they were: "Attacking in the final third of the field; making defence-splitting passes; rescuing critical situations; taking quick free kicks; making decisions about things not covered in the game plan." So invite people to agree on the following areas.

Creativity

The things people can do in a creative way are:

* ....
* ....
* ....

3) You can encourage people to continue to get the right balance between consistency and creativity.

Great teams know when to be disciplined and when to be imaginative at the defining moments. They maintain good habits – even after being knocked off course. Ask your team to tackle the final part of the exercise. First, invite people to clarify how they can continue to balance consistency and creativity in their daily work. Second, invite them to clarify how they can get the right balance during potential crises. Get them to test their conclusions by brainstorming potential problems. Exploring each event in turn, ask people to clarify how they can maintain good habits – plus add that touch of imagination – during these future difficulties.

Consistency & creativity

The things people can do to maintain the right balance of consistency & creativity in their daily work are:

* ....
* ....
* ....

The potential crisis the team may face is:

* ....

The Strengths Toolbox

The specific things people can do to balance consistency & creativity and manage this crisis successfully are:

* ....
* ....
* ....

Great teams are frequently self-managing. This calls for educating them to get the right balance between consistency and creativity. They will then be able to produce great performances when it matters.

3 tips for 'rewarding the behaviour you want repeated'

"Reward the behaviour you want repeated," is one of the basic rules of psychology. The principle applies whether you are encouraging people in a team, organisation or the wider society. Here are three tips for making this happen.

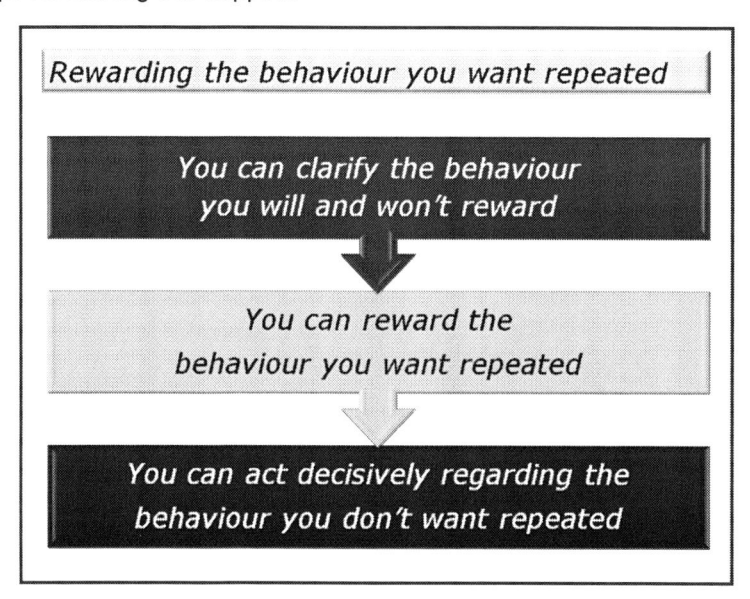

> **Rewarding the behaviour you want repeated**
>
> You can clarify the behaviour you will and won't reward
>
> ⬇
>
> You can reward the behaviour you want repeated
>
> ⬇
>
> You can act decisively regarding the behaviour you don't want repeated

1) You can clarify the behaviour you will & won't reward.

Good leaders have different personalities – but they have one thing in common. They give clear messages about how they expect people to behave. They follow this credo and are prepared to accept the consequences. Let's explore how you can take this step as a leader.

Start by clarifying the behaviour you do and don't want people to demonstrate. You may want people to take responsibility, be

The Strengths Toolbox

positive, set clear goals, encourage each other, do superb work, deliver great customer service, keep their promises or whatever. You may not want people to avoid responsibility, be negative, do poor quality work or whatever. Clarify these contrasting behaviours – then do two things. First, be a positive model. People learn from what you do, not what you say. Second, communicate the behaviour that will – and will not – be rewarded. This latter point is optional. Some leaders prefer to simply 'live the message' and, in this way, embed it into the culture. Other leaders prefer to state the rules at the outset.

I adopted the latter approach when becoming youth development officer for a football club. The players were talented but lacked discipline. For example, they argued with referees and team mates during matches. So I explained they should encourage each other and be courteous towards officials. One star player tested this in a match by arguing with the referee, so I substituted him immediately. Despite his protests, people got the message. The players learned to channel their energies in a positive way.

Imagine you are a leader who wants to set a new tone in a team or an organisation. Describe the kinds of behaviour that you will and won't reward. Try completing the following sentences.

The kinds of behaviour I do want to reward are:

* ....
* ....
* ....

The kinds of behaviour I don't want to reward are:

* ....
* ....
* ....

2) You can reward the behaviour you want repeated.

Different people encourage others in different ways. You may see somebody doing something well, for example, and have a special word with the person. Be super specific about the behaviour – or the principles – you want them to repeat. The more specific you are, the more likely people are to repeat the behaviour. When working as a football coach, at half-time I said to one winger:

"The way you beat their full back 3 times in the first half was excellent. You dummied to move in-field, changed direction to go down the right wing and put in dangerous crosses. I want you to do that again at least 5 times in the second half. It's up to you how you beat the full back. But I want you to get to the byline and put in at least 5 crosses. Is that okay?"

Companies also sometimes give clear messages about the behaviour they want people to demonstrate. Federal Express used their staff newsletter to highlight acts of 'legendary service' – such as drivers trekking across fields of snow to deliver parcels to customers. Air Miles, the loyalty card company, held corporate wide events where staff voted for and awarded valuable prizes to colleagues who 'lived the values'.

Let's return to the situation where you want to reward certain behaviour. How can you encourage people to do more of these things in the future? Try completing the following sentences.

The specific things I will do to reward the behaviour I want repeated are:

* ....
* ....
* ....

3) You can act decisively regarding the behaviour you don't want repeated.

How to act when somebody steps over the line? Each person will

The Strengths Toolbox

have their own approach, but here are the three options.

a) You can give the person a positive alternative.

You can say, for example: "In the future can you please do (a) rather than (b) The reason is _____." This gives the person a positive way forward in the future.

b) You can act immediately and practise 'zero tolerance'.

You may feel it is vital to do this if a person's behaviour contravenes a team's agreed 'rules'. It is important to 'never walk past a quality problem', otherwise you have said it is okay.

c) You can give the person a warning, outline the consequences of repeating the behaviour and be prepared to follow through.

You may believe that it is vital – and moral – to give the person another chance. The key is that you, the person and the rest of the organisation know that you are serious and will follow through. Hence some leaders practise the approach of, for example, 'three strikes and you are out'. You will pursue this approach in your own way, so try completing the following sentence.

The specific things I will do regarding the behaviour I don't want repeated are:

* ....

* ....

* ....

"Reward the behaviour you want repeated," sounds an over-simple philosophy. But I have seen it work in many situations – such as running a therapeutic community or creating a customer-focused business. People soon get the message about the desired culture and 'the way we will do things round here'.

3 tips for creating momentum by changing the physical things

Imagine you are a leader who wants to transform a culture. How can you show that working life is going be different? One approach is to learn from individuals who 'change' their lives. People can think about change for years, but the first steps often begin on a physical level. They take care of their body, start running, move house or whatever. Physical change leads to psychological change – they feel better – which reinforces the philosophical change. Let's explore how you can follow similar steps to transform a culture – 'the way we do things around here'.

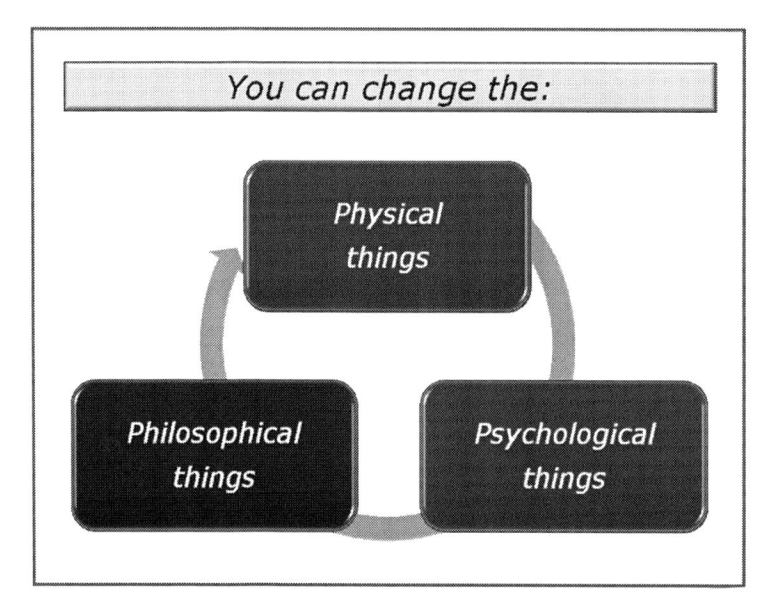

You can change the:

- Physical things
- Psychological things
- Philosophical things

1) *You can change the physical things.*

Physical changes set the tone. But they must be followed by deeper changes if you are serious about transforming a culture. 'Re-branding' by changing the airline's colours, for example, means nothing unless there are deeper changes. Start by making physical changes for the employees – beginning with the hygiene factors. Pay the market rate, improve the building and give them the tools to do the job.

"Three years ago I took over a company that was in the dark ages," said one leader. "So we modernised the entrance, gave the receptionists smart uniforms, displayed our products in the reception area, put in proper coffee bars, installed wireless and gutted the office. Previously it had been 'open plan', full of 90's style 'chicken run' desks, with little privacy. Stress and sickness were at an all time high. Redesigning the office, we got the balance between public and private spaces so people can talk or do creative work. Several Atrium areas are constantly occupied by people working or having informal meetings. They are also encouraged to work from home on Fridays. Customers now use our offices for their meetings, productivity has improved and the changes paid for themselves within one year."

People believe what they see, not what they hear. Actions speak louder than words. Change the physical things, then move onto the next step.

2) You can change the psychological things.

Create a winning feeling. When taking over a failing football team, for example, I organised a pre-season tournament with some top name clubs – teams they had only previously dreamt of playing. At the same time, however, we organised the group stages so that our club had a good chance of reaching the semi-finals. The team achieved this goal, got a medal and boosted their self-confidence. The Board were impressed and granted extra funds for buying more new players. Here are some ideas for shifting the psychological state in a culture.

Communicate the company's road map for achieving its picture of perfection. People enjoy having a sense of direction – they like a 'plan'. Put the road map in place where people can see it everyday – such as on their screen saver. Give people ownership for implementing their part of the strategy. Encourage them to get some early successes. Publicise these successes in, for example, a newsletter called 'weekly wins'. Reward the behaviour you want repeated. Promote people who live the values you want in the future culture. Spend time with the positive people. Don't pay people who choose not to opt into the new culture. Recruit new people who show the drive required to reach the team's destination.

3) You can change the philosophical things.

Great leaders harness people's energy towards achieving a compelling goal. They tap into peoples' aspirations – be it to gain freedom, deliver great customer service or create a pioneering product. Keep communicating the picture of perfection – which is the 'What'. Remind people of the 'Why' – the benefits, both for themselves and the 'customers'. Start meetings by highlighting steps that have been taken towards the goal in the past week. Show people how the philosophy is working in practice.

Why is it succeeding? They are doing something 'physically' different. They have changed the physical things to change the psychological things to change the philosophical things. Try tackling the exercise on this theme. Describe the practical things you can do under each of these 3 P's to transform 'the way we do things around here.'

Physical change

The specific things I can do to change the physical things are:

* ....
* ....
* ....

Psychological change

The specific things I can do to change the psychological things are:

* ....
* ....
* ....

Philosophical change

The specific things I can do to change the philosophical things are:

* ....
* ....
* ....

3 tips for encouraging a person to work towards the picture of perfection

Imagine you are a leader. Let's assume you have already made clear contracts about each person's contribution towards achieving the vision. How can you encourage them to keep working towards this goal? One approach is to follow a certain structure when meeting, for example, for a formal quarterly update. (Some leaders also follow this structure when having shorter, informal conversations with individuals in the coffee area.) So let's explore how you can keep people's eyes on the vision.

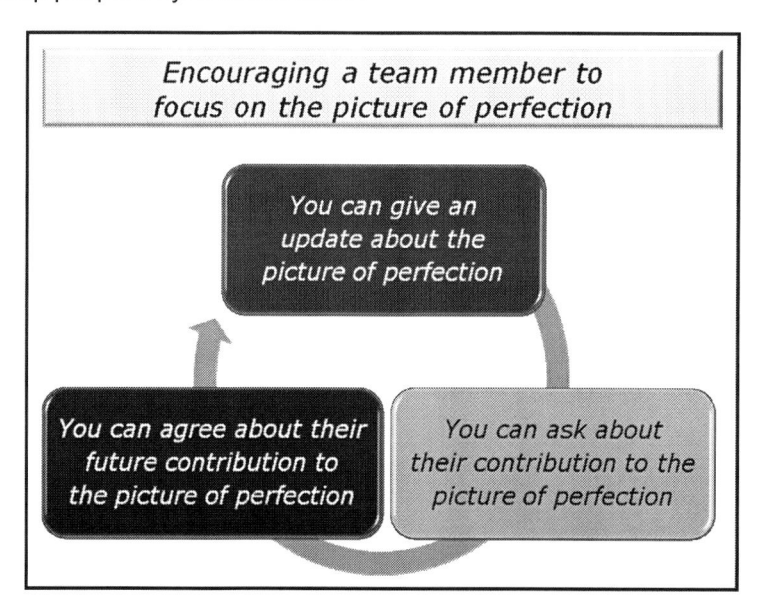

Encouraging a team member to focus on the picture of perfection

- *You can give an update about the picture of perfection*
- *You can ask about their contribution to the picture of perfection*
- *You can agree about their future contribution to the picture of perfection*

1) *You can give an update about the picture of perfection.*

Imagine you have asked a team member to meet for a quarterly update about the business. Kick off the session by describing the progress made towards the picture of perfection. You may say

167

The Strengths Toolbox

something like:

"As you know, by the end of next year we aim to achieve _____ Let me tell you how things are going in terms of the big picture. During the past three months we have achieved the following things: 1) _____ 2) _____ 3) _____ In the next three months we aim to doing the following things : 1) _____ 2) _____ 3) _____ "

Why take this approach? Great leader keep reminding people about the 'story'. Team members can get lost in their own part of the business – so giving the big picture provides a sense of meaning. People then feel they are part of something greater. You will, of course, give this overview in your own way, so try completing the following sentence.

The specific things I can do to give a person an update about the picture of perfection are:

* ....

* ....

* ....

2) You can ask about their contribution to the picture of perfection.

You can then invite the person to describe three things. (They will have obviously prepared these beforehand – but even in an informal conversation you can have a discussion around these topics.)

    a) The specific things they have done in the last three months towards achieving the POP.
    b) The specific things they plan to do in the next three months towards achieving the POP.
    c) The specific challenges they face – and the support they would like in order to achieve success.

Ask questions for information and, in your own way, compliment them on their successes. You may then want to say something like: "Is it okay if I share some ideas?" Obviously you are the boss, so they will expect you to give guidance. At the same time, however, it is good to show you are moving into a new phase of the conversation. "But shouldn't you just 'cut to the chase'?" somebody may say. "There is no point in messing around." Certainly it is vital to be direct – but the person must be open to your messages. Asking if it is okay to give input changes the 'psychological contract'. Share your ideas and ensure that both of you share the same picture. Again, you will do this in your own way, so try completing the following sentence.

The specific things I can do to ask about the person's contribution to the picture of perfection are:

* ....
* ....
* ....

3) You can agree about their future contribution to the picture of perfection.

Wrap up the conversation by making clear contracts. Agree on the person's action plans and the support required to achieve the goals. Invite them to email you summarising what has been agreed. Finally, set a date for the next formal update and, whenever possible, end the meeting in a positive way. Try completing the following sentence.

The specific things I can do to agree about the person's future contribution to the picture of perfection are:

* ....
* ....
* ....

The Strengths Toolbox

Great leaders continually go through these stages with their people. They recognise it is vital: a) To keep communicating the 'story'; b) To keep 're-centering' their people to make sure they are contributing to the story; c) To make clear contracts about people's future contribution to the story. They do it in both formal and informal meetings. Great leaders encourage their people to keep working towards the picture of perfection.

3 tips for making sure somebody completes a mission

Military analogies are not always relevant to other areas of life – but one that does resonate is that of accomplishing a 'mission'. The key to reaching the goal is to make sure that somebody 'owns' the mission. They take full responsibility for delivering the goods. Such 'accountability' is often avoided in organisations – and this means that many tasks fall through the net. Imagine you are a leader who wants several team members to work together to reach a specific goal. Here are three steps to making it happen.

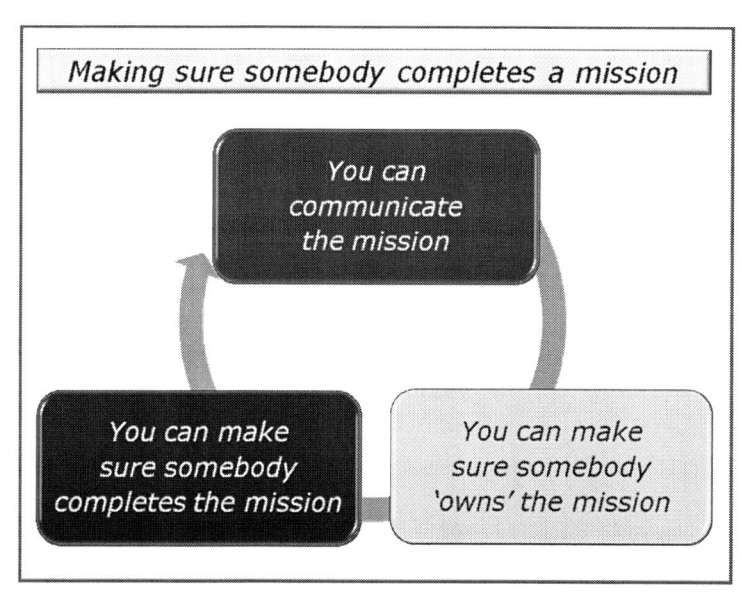

Making sure somebody completes a mission

- You can communicate the mission
- You can make sure somebody 'owns' the mission
- You can make sure somebody completes the mission

1) You can communicate the mission.

Charles Garfield, the author of *Peak Performers*, stressed the importance of communicating 'missions that motivate'. People are more likely to buy into achieving a goal if they can see the point. Great leaders bring the mission to life by outlining: a) The goals – the

'What'; b) The benefits – the 'Why'; c) The strategy for achieving the goals – the broad 'How'; d) The 'When' – when it must be accomplished. They then often ask for volunteers who want to take part – the 'Who' – because one volunteer is worth many conscripts. Imagine you want volunteers for a specific mission, such as delivering a crucial project. How can you communicate it in a compelling yet realistic way? Try completing the following exercise.

The specific things that I can do to communicate the mission are:

* ....

* ....

* ....

2) You can make sure somebody 'owns' the mission.

The message is simple. "If you want something accomplished, make sure that somebody's 'life' – or mortgage – depends on getting it done." Never give it to a committee or a group. You must have somebody who takes ownership for making it happen. Different leaders have different ways of creating this dynamic. But these often take the form of encouraging somebody to 'volunteer' for delivering the mission. You will provide all the required support, but you need one person who is accountable. Once they have stepped forward, focus on: a) Clarity – agree on crystal clear goals; b) Contracting – the 'Dos & Don'ts' involved in reaching the goals, plus the support they need to do the job; c) Concrete results – the short, medium and long-term results they will deliver by when. Try completing the following exercise.

The specific things I can do to make sure somebody takes ownership for delivering the mission are:

* ....
* ....
* ....

3) You can make sure somebody completes the mission.

Great leaders provide whatever support their people need to accomplish the mission. At the same time, they must ensure the person who is accountable also has the autonomy and authority required to do the job. This calls for a fine balancing act, but it is the only way that: a) The mission will get completed; b) The person accountable – and their team – will feel they have the freedom and power to do the job; c) The people will grow. As a leader, try completing the following sentence.

The specific things that I can do to encourage people and ensure they complete the mission are:

* ....
* ....
* ....

3 tips for being true to yourself – even if you get sacked

"There is one certainty is this job," said one leader. "There is at least a 50% chance that I will get sacked. This can be because I do not deliver the results, there is a change at the top or for some other reason. But I will be true to myself and do what I believe in. I will stand or fall by following my principles."

Imagine you are a leader taking over a team. Let's explore how you can be true to yourself in that situation.

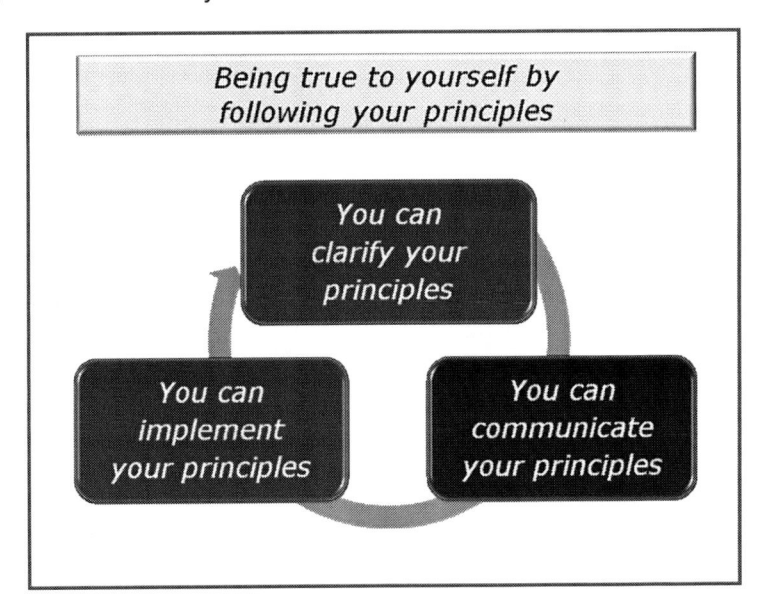

Being true to yourself by following your principles
- You can clarify your principles
- You can communicate your principles
- You can implement your principles

1) You can clarify your principles.

"I believe in following three steps towards building a successful team," said the leader mentioned above. "First, to set the right goal. This sounds simple – but it is the hardest part. Great teams set the right goal at the right time in their 'market'. Second, to build the right team. This means getting the right people in the right places, otherwise you are sunk. Third, to implement the right strategy in the right way – and keep going until you get the right results. Lots of 'rights' there – but translating these into practice takes tough decisions."

What is your philosophy for building a successful team? What are the key principles you believe in following to achieve success? Try completing the following sentence.

The key principles I believe in following to build a successful team are:

* ....
* ....
* ....

2) You can communicate your principles.

Great leaders do this in two areas. First, they communicate their principles to their sponsors before taking the role. They may say something like: "These are the results I will deliver – the 'What'. Are there any other results you would like to add?" After getting the sponsors over the emotional line where they want to 'buy' what is being offered, great leaders then say: "These are the principles I will follow to deliver the results." Whilst continually reassuring the sponsors, they outline their approach to delivering the goods. Second, they then communicate the principles to their team members. Great leaders make sure that everybody knows the 'rules'. It is then up to people to decide whether they want to contribute towards achieving the goals.

You will, of course, communicate the principles in your own way. Try completing the following sentence.

The specific things I can do to communicate these principles are:

* ....

* ....

* ....

3) *You can implement your principles.*

Great leaders relish this part. They love following their principles – especially when it comes to making tough decisions. Why? They see these as necessary for achieving success. So they make such decisions quickly to create the right foundation and keep the team on track. They then encourage, educate and enable their people to follow the daily disciplines. Sometimes, however, they come to a crunch point with their team members or sponsors.

"That has happened for me on several occasions," said the leader. "Early in my career I decided to fire a serial complainer – replacing him with a positive person. My sponsor, who I had worked for previously, backed me fully – even though I had failed to consult the HR people properly, something I learned to do in the future. Moving on to another example, I took an Operations Manager role, with the brief to spread an initiative across Europe. When it came to the crunch, however, my bosses would not back me fully. They insisted that I should try to 'influence' people, rather than have any direct authority. I soldiered on but, at best, it was only 50% successful. Since then I have learned to make clear contracts. I would sooner get sacked by being true to myself. I don't want to fail on two counts: not delivering the goods and not being true to my principles."

Let's return to your leadership role. How can implement your principles? What may be the tough decisions? How can you enable your people to deliver the goods? What may be the crunch moments in relation to your sponsors? How can you be professional and polite at such moments – yet also follow your principles? Try completing the following sentence.

The specific things I can do to implement the principles are:

* ....
* ....
* ....

Everybody encounters moments when they must make a crucial decision: do I be true to myself or do I put my principles aside for a while? Sometimes it is not 'black or white'; but ultimately it is vital to be true to yourself. Then we can laugh at Groucho Marx's joke: "Those are my principles. If you don't like them I have others."

3 tips for building on the positive energy in an organisation

How can you make change happen in an organisation? Just as importantly, how can you enjoy the process? In the old days people often got exhausted trying to shift a culture. This was partly because of the approach they took. For example, they often began by making a long list of the 'barriers to overcome'. Feeling depressed, they then tried to change the unchangeable.

Nowadays people have a different approach. Looking at the different parts of the organisation, they identify where there is positive energy and at least a 7/10 chance of success. They then do three things. First, they build on the positive energy and create successful prototypes. Second, they make tough decisions about the people and places that are not willing to develop. Third, they make the successful prototypes the model for the future organisation – and invite people to decide if they want to join this culture. They do not spend months trying to convince people to 'change'. Let's explore how you can take this route to success.

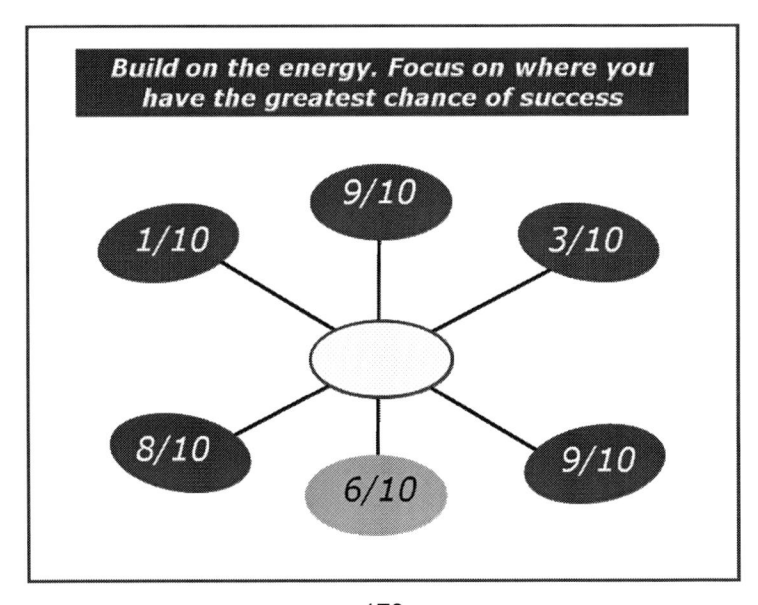

Build on the energy. Focus on where you have the greatest chance of success

- 9/10
- 1/10
- 3/10
- 8/10
- 6/10
- 9/10

1) You can identify the people and places where there is positive energy.

Tom, an incoming Managing Director, had been given the brief and mandate 'to make the company fit for the future'. Taking his senior team off-site, he began by sharing his picture of perfection. He spent a lot of time describing the positive behaviours he wanted to see people demonstrating. Certainly he could have wielded an axe, but he chose instead to build on the good things already happening. The team began by identifying:

The places & people in the organisation where there is positive energy are:

* ....
* ....
* ....

You can try this approach in your own organisation. Start by writing the names of the people who are enthusiastic. Move on to listing the places – the teams and departments – that demonstrate positive energy. Then move onto the next stage.

2) You can identify how to build on the positive energy.

Tom's leadership team brainstormed how to capitalise on these pockets of energy. Their ideas included, for example:

Giving Vicki, the customer service director, the support she needs to build a leading-edge customer service centre.

Encouraging the Danish team to build a prototype for modelling the future way of doing business with customers.

Harnessing the drive there is in the company to get involved in community work – probably teaching enterprise skills to young people in local colleges.

The Strengths Toolbox

The team listed a dozen possible 'projects', then moved on to exploring how to make these happen. Looking at your own organisation, try completing the following exercise.

The specific things we can do to build on this positive energy in the organisation are:

* ....
* ....
* ....

3) You can do everything possible to channel the positive energy towards achieving success.

Tom's team put their full weight behind the projects and helped them to deliver tangible results. The success stories were publicised using various media – articles, podcasts and the internal TV channel. Tom followed up by focusing on other places where there was positive energy. People built further successful prototypes and these became the models for the future organisation. Looking at your own organisation, try completing the following exercise.

The specific things we can do to channel the positive energy toward achieving success are:

* ....
* ....
* ....

People now know how to shift organisations. Gone are the days of getting migraines by banging their heads against brick walls. Building on the positive energy is more effective and also exciting. People go to work with a spring in their step because they know this is the way to achieve success.

3 tips for shifting a culture by building successful prototypes

Imagine you have been invited to take over a business. Your brief is to improve the results by changing the company culture. You have several options for making this happen. These include: a) You can urge everybody to 'change' and put them through a conventional 'change programme'; b) You can fire everybody and start again with a blank piece of paper; c) You can create the 'future culture' – often by building successful prototypes – and then invite people to choose whether or not they want to join this culture.

Savvy leaders often go for option (c). Why? They understand systems theory. Systems follow the law of homeostasis – they keep returning back to their present state. So don't try to change the system – create a new system with new rules. Start by building successful prototypes. The new approach can then be implemented across the company. Here are three steps towards adopting this approach.

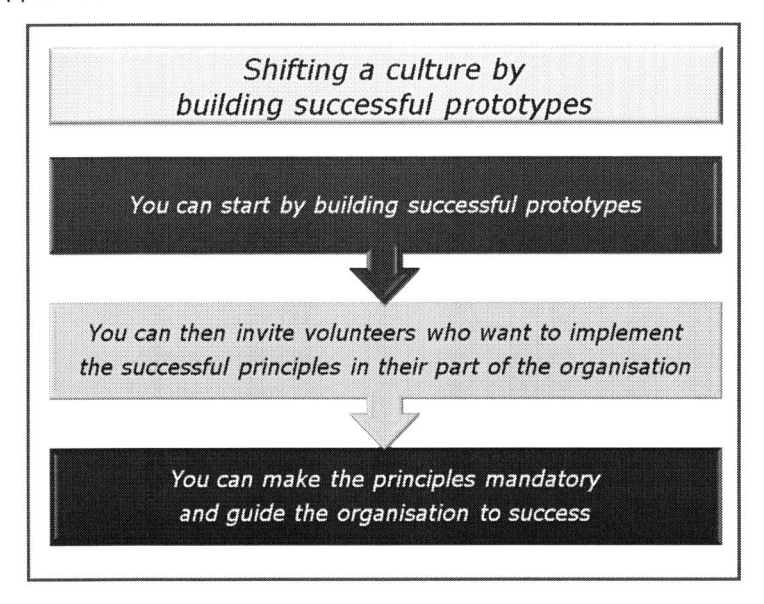

Shifting a culture by building successful prototypes

You can start by building successful prototypes

You can then invite volunteers who want to implement the successful principles in their part of the organisation

You can make the principles mandatory and guide the organisation to success

1) *You can build successful prototypes.*

Let's imagine that you want to build a company that delivers exceptional customer service. You want to begin by building prototypes that demonstrate this approach. Here are some steps towards making it happen.

- **You can set up the prototypes to succeed.**

Looking around the different departments, rate the chances of success of running such a pilot. Go with the positive energy. Clarify where the chances are at least 7/10 – then choose where you will build the prototypes. Another option is to go for a 'Green Field' site: a new site with new people who will adopt a new approach.

- **You can appoint the right people, make clear contracts and give them the support they need to succeed.**

Get the right people in place – especially good leaders – otherwise you are sunk. Clarify 'What' they must deliver by 'When'. Outline the broad principles of the 'How', but they must be given freedom, within parameters, to implement the strategy. Give them the support they need to do the job.

- **You can 'ring fence' the prototypes in order to help them to succeed.**

Why? Sometimes old systems try to stop new ones from succeeding, so provide protection. Companies sometimes give double messages, such as: "We want you to be bright, creative and deliver results in the new world. We also want you to follow the old rules to achieve these results."

- **You can encourage people to get some early wins – but also create an 'event' for showcasing the prototypes' success.**

Encourage people to get some early wins to build positive momentum and publicise these across the business. Set a date for a company event in 6 months time where they will present their success stories. Sounds challenging, but people respond to deadlines.

- **You can do everything possible to ensure the prototypes are successful.**

You can provide an inspiring vision, but it is up to the prototype-builders to do the work. Keep in touch with them, but in a supportive way. Ask: "What do you want from me to help you to be successful?" Then, wherever possible, provide that support. Explain how you want to be kept updated – because you need a reality check – and how they can keep you off their backs! Encourage them to communicate their achievements along the road and also celebrate success. If things go wrong, however, make the tough decisions early, rather than late.

- **You can get people to present the lessons from the successful prototypes.**

Success provides its own arguments – so publicise the success stories. People can do this through newsletters, articles, internal television, DVD's or whatever. Then move onto the next stage.

2) *You can invite volunteers who want to implement the successful principles in their part of the business.*

People are more likely to adopt new behaviour if they see the benefits. Imagine you have backed several prototypes that have delivered exceptional customer service. Arrange a company event – or other communication vehicles – where the prototype-builders present: a) The principles that have proved successful; b) The things we learned and can do better next time. You can then announce the next phase by saying something like:

"The prototypes have shown how we can deliver exceptional customer service. We are looking for volunteers who want to follow these principles in their part of the business. The goal will be to achieve customer satisfaction ratings of at least 98% – and this can be to either your external or internal customers. Get back to me within one week to let me know: a) Whether you want to deliver this 'What'; b) 'How', in broad terms, you aim to deliver it; c) The support you need to do the job. This obviously means a shift in culture –

changing the way we do things around here. We can succeed with this new approach, so let me know if you want to be part of making it happen."

Great leaders communicate a compelling story. They show the benefits and also explain the Dos and Don'ts for reaching the goal. They then give people the chance to opt in – because they believe in working with volunteers, not victims. You will pursue this path in your own way. Give people the required support and showcase the new success stories. Then move onto the final step.

3) You can make the principles mandatory and guide the organisation to success.

You have backed successful prototypes that embody the future culture. Now it is the time for people to make a decision. So you may give them the following message.

"The prototypes have shown the principles we must follow to be successful. The pluses are that we will improve our services and stay in business. The minuses are that it will be challenging, especially at first. But it is the way to build a successful future. What I am saying to you is also challenging. I am asking you to decide whether or not you want to follow those principles. If so, get back to your manager within the next week and we will agree on how you want to contribute. If we do not hear from you, we will assume you want to move on. So we will then try to work out, as far as possible, a 'win-win'. This may be a tough message, but we must follow these principles to achieve success. Let me or your manager know if you want to contribute to the journey."

Sounds challenging – but frequently there is no other option. People must decide whether or not they want to be part of the future culture. Expect some rocky times, but eventually things will work out. You will have laid the foundations by building the prototypes. Keep people's eyes on the picture of perfection. Reward the behaviour you want repeated. Be prepared to make tough decisions. Never walk past a quality problem – otherwise you have said it is okay. Maintain the momentum by continuing to publicise success stories. Do whatever is necessary to guide the organisation to success. If you wish, try tackling this exercise that invites you to translate these principles into action.

The specific things I can do to build successful prototypes are:

* ....
* ....
* ....

The specific things I can do to invite volunteers who want to implement the successful principles are:

* ....
* ....
* ....

The specific things I can do to make the principles mandatory and guide the organisation to success are:

* ....
* ....
* ....

3 tips for inviting your team to answer the 'rolling contract' question

Imagine you are a leader. You have a good team, but they need to become even more customer-focused. People need to recognise that, in the new world of work, 'there are no jobs anymore; there are only projects'. They are only as good as their present project and the success they deliver. Here is an exercise you can use to encourage the individuals – and the whole team – to demonstrate even more professionalism.

The 'rolling contract' question

If you were on a 6 month rolling contract that had to be signed-off every month by your key sponsors, how would you behave?

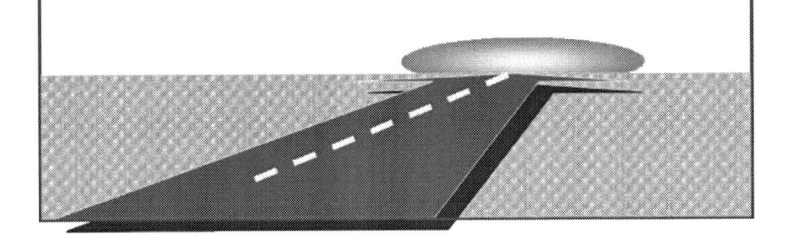

1) You can invite the team to answer the 'rolling contract' question.

Gather the team together and ask them to tackle the 'Rolling Contract' exercise. You may want to say something like:

"Imagine we have each put £100k into the kitty and this team is our own business. We have got a 6 month contract with our present organisation. But there is a challenge. This is a 6 month 'rolling contract' that must be signed off – extended – every month by our key sponsors. How would we behave? Knowing the contract could come to an end in 6 months, would we behave any differently? Remember, it is our money and our mortgages. Would we get closer to our sponsors, make clearer contracts, report successes, anticipate future challenges – and business opportunities – or whatever? Take 15 minutes to brainstorm what we would do if we were on a 6 month rolling contract."

The specific things we would do if we were on a rolling contract would be:

* ....
* ....
* ....

2) You can implement the ideas that emerge from the 'rolling contract' question.

Gather all the suggestions, sort these into themes and discuss what has emerged. Looking at the ideas, settle on those the team want to implement. Consider the pluses and minuses of pursuing these strategies. Build on the pluses and minimise the minuses. Get 'owners' for the actions. Provide the necessary support and encourage people to get some quick successes. Repeat the 'rolling contract' question during team meetings and one-to-one sessions. So invite people to complete the following sentences.

The specific ideas that we can implement now are:

* ....
* ....
* ....

The Strengths Toolbox

The benefits of doing these things will be:

* ....
* ....
* ....

3) You can encourage individuals to consider what they personally would do if they were on a 'rolling contract'.

Great teams are made up of people who take responsibility and are committed to constant improvement. If appropriate, ask each person: "If you were on a 6 month rolling contract – that had to be signed off every month – how would you behave?" Even the most professional person will find some ways to improve their performance. Encourage them to translate these ideas into action.

Institutions frequently give double messages. On the one hand they say: "Be quick, agile and think for yourself." On the other hand they say: "Let us do the thinking for you." People can become inward facing and lose the ability to live off their wits. The 'rolling contract' question aims to re-ignite their sense of urgency and increase their customer focus.

3 tips for communicating your team's story

Great teams communicate a compelling story. They have one story – not six different stories – though it can expressed in many ways. Everybody in the team can bring the story to life with examples that resonate with different audiences. Imagine you are a leader. You want to involve your people in clarifying and communicating the team's story. Let's explore how you can make this happen.

Communicating the team's story

You can enable the team to go through the following steps

- You can clarify the story
- You can practice communicating the story
- You can communicate the story

1) You can clarify the story.

Create half a day to meet with your team. Start by making sure that people are crystal clear on the team's overall strategy. Ensure everybody knows the 'What, Why, How, Who & When'. This is the overall team strategy/story – so it is rather long. People will later learn how to summarise and bring it to life. One point is worth bearing in mind. It is good to have an inspiring 'one-line' goal. This captures what the team is trying to achieve and should, if possible, appeal to both the heart and the head. So here are the topics that everybody should be clear on regarding the team's strategy.

The 'What'

The goal we want to achieve by _____ is:

- To _____

The specific things that will be happening then that will show we have reached the goals will be:

- _____
- _____
- _____

The 'Why'

The benefits of reaching the goals will be:

For the company

- _____
- _____

For the customers

- _____
- _____

For the colleagues

- _____
- _____

The 'How'

The key strategies we will follow to achieve the goals are:

- To _____
  _____

- To _____
  _____

- To _____
  _____

The 'Who'

*The leadership team's responsibilities
in working to achieve the goals are:*

- _____

*The managers' responsibilities
in working to achieve the goals are:*

- _____

*The colleagues' responsibilities
in working to achieve the goals are:*

- _____

> ## The 'When' – The Road Map
>
> *Some of the specific things that will be happening along the road towards achieving the goals will be:*
>
> - _____
> - _____
> - _____
> - _____

2) You can practise communicating the story.

Now comes the fun part. Invite people to spend time clarifying their 'elevator pitch'. They must be able to summarise the story and bring it to life for a particular audience. So ask them to spend 15 minutes putting together their summary of the story. They are to cover the following areas. (See exercise on the next page.)

- **The target group & the situation.**

They are to choose the target group to whom they wish to communicate the story. It can be colleagues, partners, customers, venture capitalists, friends or whatever. They are also to decide on the situation in which they are telling the story.

- **The 'What'.**

They are to describe the team's goal. As we mentioned earlier, it is good to have an agreed 'one-liner' that capture's the team's aim and appeals to both the heart and the head.

- **The 'How'.**

They are to describe – in headline form – the key strategies for achieving the goal. Depending on the audience, sometimes it can be good to give a bit more detail on these strategies, but not go into long explanations. After all, it is an elevator pitch.

- **Bringing the story to life.**

They are to bring the story to life by giving real examples of what the story looks like in practice. The illustrations must be relevant for their chosen audience and, hopefully, also highlight the benefits.

Give two guidelines regarding the way they communicate the story. a) Everybody should communicate the big 'What' and 'How'. b) Everybody should then use their own personalities and examples to illustrate the story and make it relevant for their chosen audience. Here is the exercise.

The story

The target audience and the specific situation where I will be telling the story is:

* ....

Here is what I will actually say to people.

*The **'What'**. The goal we are aiming to achieve is:*

* ....

*The **'How'**. The key things we will do to achieve the goal are:*

* ....

* ....

* ....

The Strengths Toolbox

Bringing it to life.

Here is an example that shows what it means in practice.

* ....

Give people around 15 minutes to complete the written part. Then invite them to read their summary of the story. Each person is to begin by setting the scene, explaining the target group and situation. They are then to communicate the story – *as if they are talking to their chosen audience*. Continue until everybody has finished.

You may wish to comment on the contributions. Normally there is lots of commonality, but people find their own ways to bring it to life. Explain to people that, whilst the process may still feel a bit 'wooden', they will eventually find the story comes more naturally. They may also reach the stage where they start moving the sequence around. For instance, depending on the audience, they may start with the real life examples, then link those to the 'What' and 'How'. People quickly reach a level of consistency with the story, yet are also able to use their own personalities. It is then time to move onto the next stage.

Tough questions can throw a spanner in the works, so educate your people how to deal with such problems. Invite each person to brainstorm ideas under the following headings.

Tough questions

The possible tough questions that people may ask are:

* ....

The answers I can give to this question are:

* ....

* ....

* ....

Give people the opportunity to share their 'tough questions' and possible answers. Make sure everybody is happy that all topics have been covered. Then move onto the next stage.

3) *You can communicate the story.*

Be clear on how you want to share the story with colleagues, customers and the wider public. You may want to use road shows, internal meetings, media interviews, newsletters and corporate events. Do this in a compelling and, where possible, involving way. One MD explained:

"My first six months in this role were spent focusing on the systems – making sure we delivered. I then realised we had a great 'machine', but little magic. So I spent the next few months communicating our story. I visited every team in the business to hold 'unplugged' sessions, tell the story and answer tough questions. People began to believe in our purpose and translated it into positive results. The hard part was reminding myself to continue communicating the story. This is something that has to be done every day, every week, every month. It is the best way to breathe life into a company."

How can your team communicate the story? How can they keep it alive? Try completing the following sentences.

The specific things we can do to communicate the story are:

* ....
* ....
* ....

The specific things we can do to keep the story alive are:

* ....
* ....
* ....

The Strengths Toolbox

Great teams have one story – not six stories. You can encourage, educate and enable your team to keep communicating the story. This will then become the heartbeat of the business.

Sharing knowledge

3 tips for clarifying what you can offer as a mentor

Imagine somebody has asked you to be their mentor. You want to help them, but are not sure what you can offer. Here are three things you can do before the first session.

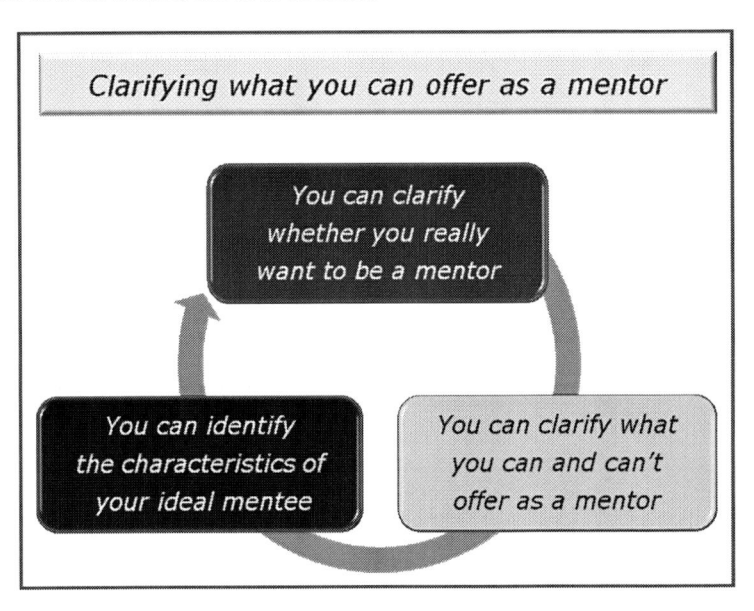

Clarifying what you can offer as a mentor

- You can clarify whether you really want to be a mentor
- You can clarify what you can and can't offer as a mentor
- You can identify the characteristics of your ideal mentee

1) You can clarify whether you really want to be a mentor.

Mentors are wise and trusted advisers. They pass on knowledge in a way that helps the mentee to achieve their personal or professional goals. Good mentoring calls for being prepared to spend quality time with the mentee. The frequency of the meetings can be worked out together, but you may need to set aside at least 2-3 hours every quarter. Try completing the following sentence.

On a scale 0 – 10, the extent to which I feel motivated to be a mentor is: ____ / 10

Make sure the motivation is at least 8/10. Assuming you are ready to make the necessary commitment, move onto the next step.

2) You can clarify what you can & can't offer as a mentor.

Try tackling the exercise called *Mentoring: What I can & can't offer*. One person wrote: "I can offer the mentee time; encouragement; an overview of their situation; problem-solving skills and knowledge of this organisation. I can't offer magic solutions or do the work for them." Try completing the following sentences.

The things I can offer as a mentor are:

* ....
* ....
* ....
* ....

The things I can't offer as a mentor are:

* ....
* ....
* ....
* ....

3) You can clarify the characteristics of your ideal mentee.

Frequently we ask mentees to clarify the qualities they want in their ideal mentor. Similarly, it is important for the mentor to understand

The Strengths Toolbox

the kind of mentee with whom they work best. One mentor wrote: "I like working with somebody who is positive, hungry and intuitive. For example, they like learning from many different fields, such as business, the arts and sports. I also work best with people in the 'newer' industries. Such people like to write the new rules, rather than be straitjacketed by the old ones." Tackle the exercise on this theme called *My ideal mentee.* Try completing the following sentence.

The characteristics of my ideal mentee is somebody who:

* ....

* ....

* ....

* ....

You will then be ready to go onto the next step – facilitating the actual mentoring session.

3 tips for facilitating a mentoring session

How can you facilitate a mentoring session? One approach is to follow the classic '5C' model which is based on creative problem-solving. This encourages the mentee to focus on their challenges, choices, consequences, creative solutions and conclusions. Let's explore how you can follow these steps in your own way.

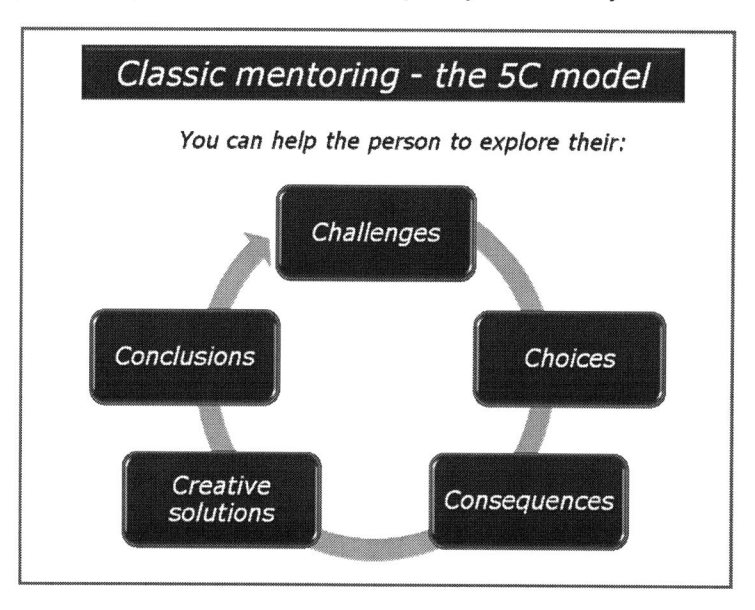

Classic mentoring - the 5C model

You can help the person to explore their:

- Challenges
- Choices
- Consequences
- Creative solutions
- Conclusions

1) You can welcome the person, create a stimulating sanctuary and, when appropriate, explore their first challenge.

Good mentors begin by making the person feel welcome and creating a stimulating sanctuary. They then establish what the person wants to explore during the session. You will do this in your own way – but here are some questions you can ask to clarify the person's agenda.

"What are the topics you would like to explore? What for you would make it a successful session? Looking at these various themes, which is the first challenge you would like to tackle? Can you give some background and explain what is happening at the moment? What is it you can and can't control in this situation? Looking at the challenge, what are the *real results* you want to achieve? If there are several results you want to achieve, let's put these in order of priority. What are your specific goals? What is your picture of perfection? Let's be crystal clear on the 'What' before moving onto the 'How'."

Bearing these questions in mind, you may get to the point where the person frames the challenge in the following way.

The challenge I want to tackle is:

*How to ....

*The **real results** I want to achieve are:*

*To ....

*To ....

*To ....

2) *You can clarify their choices, consequences and creative solutions.*

Good mentors help the person to explore their choices – the possible options for tackling the challenge. They then move onto the consequences – the pluses and minuses of each option. Finally during this stage, they help the person to consider possible creative solutions. Again, you will do this in your own way, but here are some trigger questions you may ask the person at each stage.

"Let's consider the possible choices you have for tackling this challenge. What do you see as Option A? (Doing nothing is, of course, an option.) What is Option B; Option C; Option D; Option E? What other strategies have you tried before? Are there any other possible options?

Sharing Knowledge

"Let's consider the consequences of each option. What are the pluses and minuses involved in pursuing Option A; Option B; Option C; Option D; Option E? We will soon be exploring potential creative solutions, but first let's check your gut feeling for each of the possibilities. Rate the attractiveness of each option. Do this on a scale 0–10.

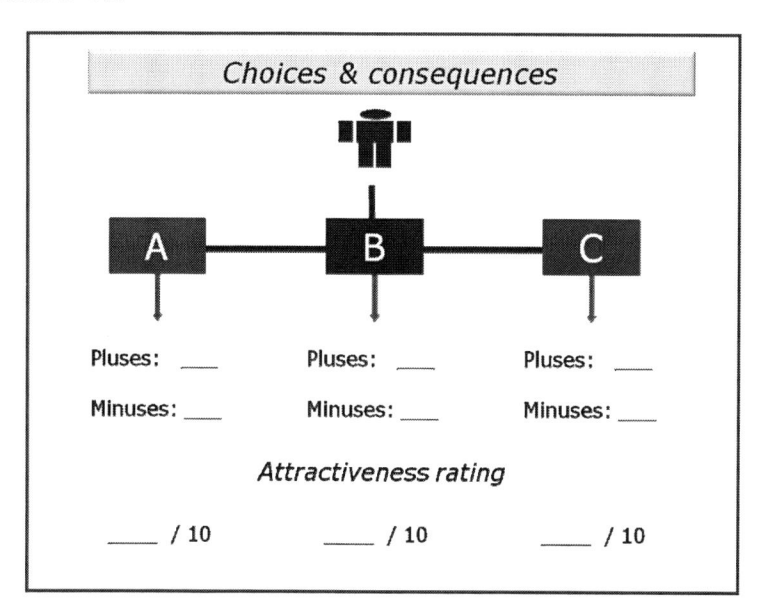

Choices & consequences

A	B	C
Pluses: ___	Pluses: ___	Pluses: ___
Minuses: ___	Minuses: ___	Minuses: ___

Attractiveness rating

___ / 10   ___ / 10   ___ / 10

"Let's move onto the possible creative solutions. First, let's re-establish your goals. What are the **real** results you want to achieve? Looking at the different options you have outlined: Is it possible to take the best parts from each option and create a new road? Let's learn from your successful history. Have you ever been in a similar situation in the past and managed it successfully? What did you do right? How can you follow these paths again in the future? Looking at the challenge: Are there any other possible creative solutions?"

Good mentors move onto sharing any ideas, tools and models the mentee can use to achieve success. They pass on this knowledge in a way the mentee can accept and check out which ideas resonate. You will do this in your own way and continue until the mentee is ready to move onto the next stage.

3) You can help the person to clarify their conclusions.

There is often a natural rhythm to a mentoring session. You will encourage the mentee to explore the first challenge, choices and consequences. After considering the potential creative solutions, the mentee reflects and then, at a certain point, will be ready to move onto the final stage – their conclusions. They settle on their plan for tackling the challenge. When it feels appropriate, you can enable them to take this step by using some of the following questions.

"Looking at the different options we have discussed, which route do you want to travel? What will be the pluses and minuses of pursuing this option? Are you prepared to accept the whole package? Let's move on to your action plan. What steps must you take to reach your goals? How can you make this happen? Momentum is vital, so how can you get an early success? You can only do your best, of course, and make sure you also have a back-up plan. What is the next challenge you want to tackle?"

You will have your own style of facilitating a mentoring session – but the 5C model can be a useful approach to add to your repertoire. Here is the complete framework that you can use in the session.

Challenges

The challenge I want to tackle is:

*How to ....

The real results I want to achieve are:

*To ....

*To ....

*To ....

Sharing Knowledge

Choices

The possible options I have are:

a) To ....

b) To ....

c) To...

Consequences

The pluses & minuses of each option are:

a) To ....

Pluses: ....

Minuses: ....

Attractiveness: ____ /10

b) To ....

Pluses: ....

Minuses: ....

Attractiveness: ____ /10

c) To...

Pluses: ....

Minuses: ....

Attractiveness: ____ /10

Creative solutions

The possible creative solutions are:

*To ....

*To ....

*To ....

Conclusions

The route – or routes – I want to take is:

*To ....

3 tips for establishing a coaching contract

Imagine that somebody has asked you to be their coach. Before embarking on the coaching process it is vital to establish their goals. Setting specific targets increases the likelihood of success. Here are three suggestions for clarifying the coaching contract. (While the following process sounds very structured, you can do it in your own way. It will provide the basis for building a successful coaching relationship.)

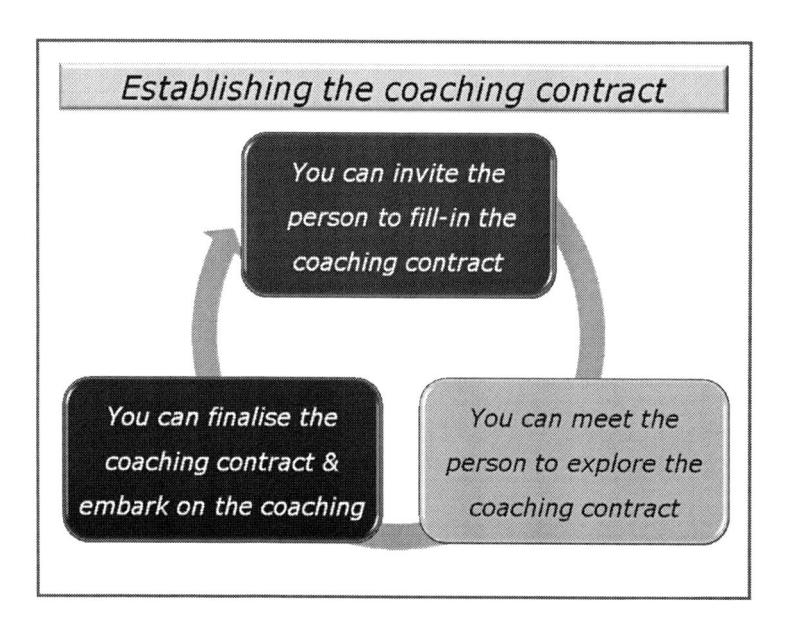

Establishing the coaching contract

- You can invite the person to fill-in the coaching contract
- You can meet the person to explore the coaching contract
- You can finalise the coaching contract & embark on the coaching

1) You can invite the person to fill in the coaching contract.

You may well start by having an informal conversation with the person. Certainly they will have dreams – but it is vital to discover if they have the desire and discipline required to deliver. Clear contracting is vital in any relationship – and this is especially so between the coach and the learner. Before meeting for a second time, you may find it useful to invite them to complete the coaching contract.

The person is asked to describe: a) The specific goals they want to achieve. b) My role: the things they see as their responsibility in achieving the goals. c) The coach's role: the help they want from the coach. d) The measures: the things that will show they have reached the goals. The person is to send the contract to you ahead of the second session. You can gauge their attitude and aspirations by the amount of work they put into creating the contract. Here is the framework that is to be filled in by the learner.

Coaching contract

The specific goals. The specific goals I want to achieve are:

* ....
* ....
* ....

My role. The things I see as my responsibility in working to achieve these goals are:

* ....
* ....
* ....

The coach's role. The knowledge, tools and support I would like from the coach are:

* ....
* ....
* ....

The measures. *The specific things that will be happening that will show I have reached the goals are:*

* ....

* ....

* ....

2) You can meet with the person to explore the coaching contract.

Set aside at least an hour to discuss the contract in depth. Invite them to explain what they see as their responsibility in the relationship. Move onto discussing the help they want from you as a coach. Encourage them to consider the challenges on the way – including potential setbacks – and how they plan to deal with these situations. Conclude this part of the session by asking them to describe their success criteria – the things that will show they have reached their goals. Providing you are happy, move onto the next stage.

3) You can finalise the coaching contract and, if appropriate, embark on the actual coaching.

Create a short 'time out' to enable the person to reflect and make any alterations to the contract. Time permitting – and if appropriate – you may then both want to launch into the actual coaching. If so, invite the person to explore the first topic they want to tackle. You can help them: a) To build on their strengths; b) To learn tools for tackling areas for improvement; c) To do what is necessary to achieve success. Conclude the session by asking them to clarify what they have learned and inviting them to do any relevant homework before the next meeting. Finally, evaluate your own performance. Describe: a) Three things I did well in the session; b) Two things I can do better in the future – and how. Relax, reflect and then look forward to the next session.

The Strengths Toolbox

The coaching contract may sound quite formal. But you can adapt it in your own way to make sure everybody is clear on the goals and mutual responsibilities. This creates a good framework for working together successfully.

3 tips for being a good encourager

Everybody needs encouragement. So how can you be a good encourager? How can you help a person to become the best kind of artist, engineer, teacher or whatever they want to be? How can you discover what gives them energy? How can you help them to excel? Good encouragers are like good educators. They focus on the three E's: encouragement, enterprise and excellence. Let's explore how you can follow these steps when helping another person.

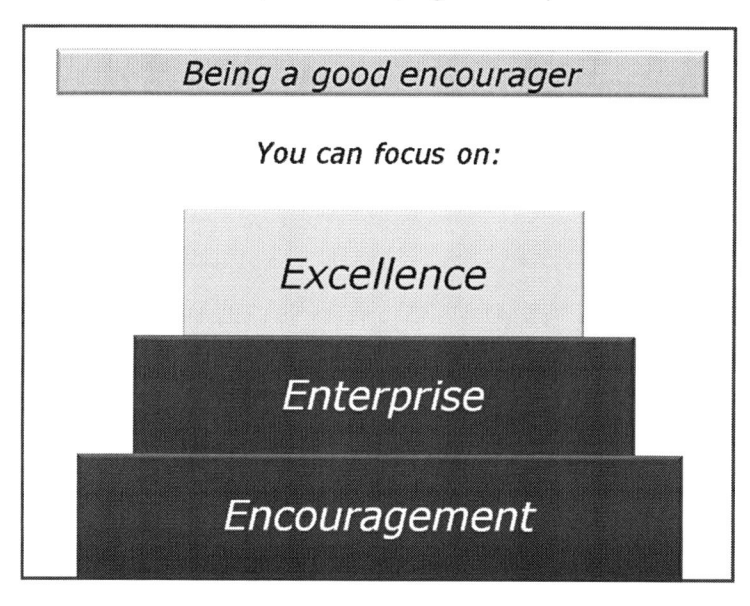

Being a good encourager

You can focus on:

- Excellence
- Enterprise
- Encouragement

1) *You can focus on encouragement.*

Encouragement often starts on a basic level. The first stage calls for providing people with practical support, such as the materials for life -food, shelter and the ability to shape their future. The second stage calls for offering people psychological support. So how can you provide individuals with such encouragement?

Try tackling the exercise on this theme called *My encouragers*. This invites you to do three things. First, looking back on your life, write the names of 3 people who have encouraged you. For example, a parent, teacher, sports coach, manager, friend, writer, artist or whoever. Second, describe what they did right to be good encouragers. For example, they may have made you feel the centre of the world, identified your talents and, when necessary, given tough messages. Third, bearing these principles in mind, describe how you can encourage other people. Everybody is different, of course, so it is obviously important to check with them how they want to be encouraged.

My Encouragers

Some of the encouragers I have had in my life have been:

1)..

The specific things this person did to encourage me were:

* ....
* ....
* ....

2)..

The specific things this person did to encourage me were:

* ....
* ....
* ....

3) ....

   The specific things this person did to encourage me were:

   * ....

   * ....

   * ....

Bearing these answers in mind, the principles I can follow to encourage people are:

* ....

* ....

* ....

My action plan. *The specific things I therefore want to do to encourage other people are:*

* ....

* ....

* ....

2) You can focus on enterprise.

Good encouragers are like good educators. Looking at a person, they ask themselves: "When does the person 'come alive'? When do they take initiatives? What are the activities in which they are 'in their element'? When do they show a sense of enterprise?" George Lyward, a pioneer in child care, used to say: "You have to look for what Antoine St. Exupery called 'The Murdered Mozart' in each person. Look for the golden moments when they become fascinated by an activity. A person may be painting, playing football or whatever. Help them to discover what they are doing right. Help them to find and follow their natural discipline. They can then create more of those golden moments. Help the person to become the best kind of Mozart they can be."

3) *You can focus on excellence.*

Good educators build on a person's positive energy and help them to achieve excellence. They agree with the person on: a) The goals they want to achieve: b) The person's role in achieving the goals: c) The help they want from the educator. They then work together to enable the person to achieve excellence. If appropriate, you can follow similar principles to help somebody to reach their goals. Try tackling the following exercise. Start by identifying a particular person you want to encourage, then do three things. First, describe the specific things you can to do encourage them. Second, describe the things you can do to look for when they show enterprise. Third, describe the things you can do – if appropriate – to help them to achieve excellence.

The specific person I want to encourage is:

* ....

The specific things I can do to encourage them are:

* ....

* ....

* ....

The specific things I can do to look for and then build on where they show enterprise are:

* ....

* ....

* ....

Sharing Knowledge

The specific things I can then do to – if appropriate – help them to achieve excellence are:

* ....

* ....

* ....

Certainly this approach works if you are in a professional relationship, such as acting as a manager, mentor or coach. Personal relationships have a different dynamic – and it is important not to automatically move into a 'coaching role'. There is nothing more annoying than somebody who tries to fix everybody else's life! Sometimes it can be appropriate, however, to encourage a person along their road towards achieving excellence. Encouragers are on the side of life. They keep planting seeds of hope and we never forget a good encourager.

3 tips for building on a person's strengths

Everybody is an artist, everybody is creative, everybody has something special to give to the world. So how can you find a person's talents? Here are three sets of questions you can use to help them to find their strengths, set specific goals and achieve success.

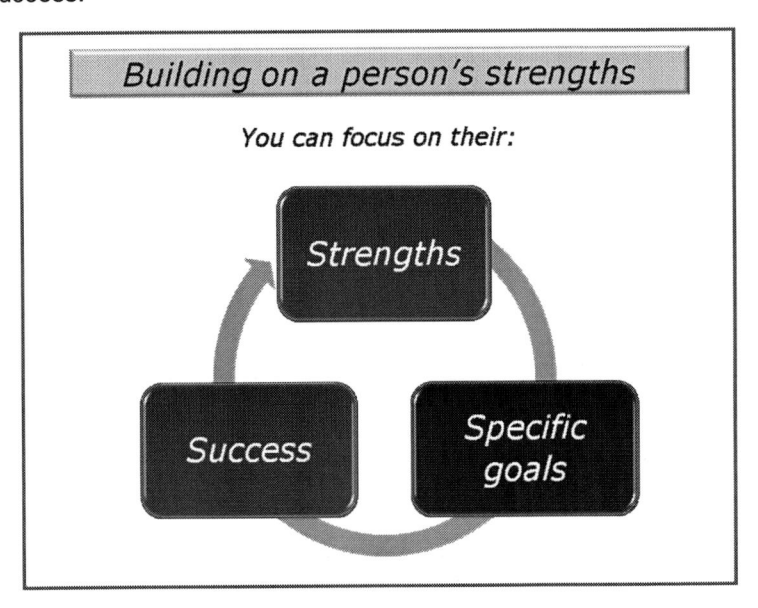

Building on a person's strengths
You can focus on their:

- Strengths
- Specific goals
- Success

1) *You can focus on the person's strengths.*

Everybody can find activities in which they quickly reach 7/10. The challenge is to find a niche in which they consistently deliver at least 9/10. So how can you help a person to identify their 'A' talent? One approach is to focus on three themes. a) Their strengths – 'What' they do best. b) Their successful style – 'How' they work best. c) They can then combine their strengths and successful style to clarify their special contribution. You can help a person to clarify their talents by asking questions such as:

"What are the activities in which you deliver 'As', rather than 'Bs' or 'Cs'? When do you feel in your element – you feel at ease at yet also excel? When do you quickly see the destination – the picture of perfection? When do you go 'a, b … then jump to … z'? Where do you quickly see patterns? When do you flow, focus, finish and, as a by-product, find fulfilment? How do you work best? Looking back on your life, describe what for you have been satisfying 'projects'. What for you made them satisfying? Can you see any patterns? How can you combine your strengths and successful style to clarify your special contribution?"

Imagine you are planning to help a person to develop their talents. Try completing the following sentence.

The specific things I can do to help a person to find their strengths are:

* ....
* ....
* ....

2) You can focus on the person's specific goals.

Everybody can set specific goals. So how can you help a person to clarify their picture of perfection? If they feel it would be useful, you can focus on three themes. a) They can set specific goals. b) They can, if appropriate, find potential sponsors. (A sponsor is somebody who may hire them for doing what they do best.) c) They can clarify their strategy for achieving their specific goals. You can help them to take these steps by asking questions such as:

"What is your picture of success? Imagine you are looking back at your life when you are 80. What will be the three things you will have done that will mean your life has been successful? What is your picture of perfection? If you want to get paid for doing what you love, how can you find potential sponsors? What are the key challenges they face? How can you use your strengths to help them to achieve success? Once you have found potential sponsors, how can you

The Strengths Toolbox

make clear contracts with them? Returning to your long-term picture of perfection, what are the three key things you can do to give yourself the greatest chance of success?"

Let's return to the person you are planning to encourage. Try completing the follow sentence.

The specific things I can do to help a person to set specific goals are:

* ....

* ....

* ....

3) *You can focus on the person's success.*

Everybody can work hard to achieve their picture of success. Peak performers, for example, develop good habits and do the right things in the right way every day. Overcoming setbacks along the way, they work hard until they reach their goals. Sometimes they also add that 'touch of class'. Here are three steps the person may wish to consider on their own journey. a) They can do superb work. b) They can find solutions to challenges. c) They can achieve their picture of success. How to help them to chart their route toward their goals? You can ask questions such as:

"How can you do superb work? How can you follow the daily disciplines? How can you satisfy your sponsors? How can you encourage yourself along the journey? How can you anticipate and manage any setbacks? How can you find creative solutions to challenges? How can you stay proactive? How can you keep tackling issues that are in the green, amber and red zones? How can you be a good finisher? How can you do everything possible to achieve your picture of perfection? How can you then add that touch of class? How can you keep improving? How can you find the next satisfying project?"

Let's conclude by returning to the person you want to encourage. Conclude the exercise by completing the following sentence.

Sharing Knowledge

The specific things I can do to help a person to achieve success are:

* ....

* ....

* ....

3 tips for clarifying a person's will to reach their goal

"Will plus skill can thrill," is a phrase people use in sport. So how does this apply in other situations? Imagine that you have been asked to coach a person, but you are not sure whether they are motivated. It can be good to establish their attitude before embarking on the coaching. The key question to answer is:

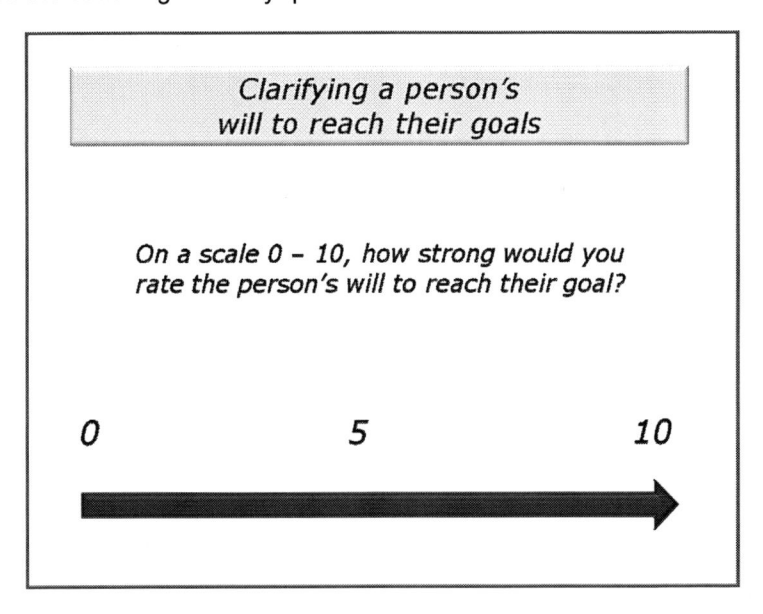

> **Clarifying a person's will to reach their goals**
>
> *On a scale 0 – 10, how strong would you rate the person's will to reach their goal?*
>
> 0　　　　　5　　　　　10
> ──────────────▶

Let's consider how you can explore this factor.

1) You can clarify whether the person is willing to put in the hard work required to reach their goal.

Clarify whether the person is prepared to work hard to reach their goal. You can, for example, invite them to fill in and send you the 'Coaching Contract'. (See the piece called *3 tips for establishing a coaching contract*.) This asks the person to describe: a) The goals they want to achieve; b) Their responsibility in working towards achieving the goals; c) The help they want from you as the coach; d) The measures that will tell them they have reached their goals. Completing this contract shows the person is willing to put in lots of work just to get to first base.

2) You can clarify the person's will to accept the pluses and minuses involved in reaching the goal.

This is a vital but often overlooked part of working with people. Looking at the goal they want to achieve, invite the person to list *what they see* as the pluses and minuses involved. One way to illustrate this, for example, is to consider the challenges facing a drug addict who wants to 'change their life'. Looking at it from the addict's point of view:

The pluses will be:
- They will live longer.
- They will possibly build better relationships.
- They will possibly like themselves more.
- They may feel in more control.

The possible minuses will be:
- They must take responsibility every day for the rest of their lives.
- They must find a new purpose – other than getting a fix.
- They must work to get money.
- They must make new friends.
- They must deal with their feeling without drugs.

The drug addict's odyssey is one example – but every person's journey will involve upsides and downsides. Let's return to the person you are trying to encourage. Are they prepared to accept the whole package – the pluses and minuses involved in reaching their goal?

3) You can clarify the person's will to keep working hard after they have achieved success.

This is crucial when, for example, working with rising sports stars. Some athletes develop a pattern of almost reaching their target – winning a tennis title, golf championship or whatever – but failing when the prize is in sight. Certainly it can be due to circumstances, such as facing an outstanding competitor – but there can be other reasons. Subconsciously the person may feel:

"What happens if I win? Everybody will expect me to keep winning in the future. Am I prepared to give up my social life? Am I prepared to put in the hard work necessary to continue being successful?"

Some athletes answer 'Yes'. Others are more uncertain and this shows in their performance. Clarify whether the person is ready to keep growing after their first triumph. Try completing the following sentences.

The things I can do to establish a person's will to achieve their goal are:

* ....

* ....

* ....

The things I can do to establish a person's will to accept the pluses & minuses involved in reach their goal are:

* ....

* ....

* ....

Sharing Knowledge

The things I can do to establish a person's will to keep working hard after they have achieved success are:

* ....
* ....
* ....

After establishing a person's will, help them to learn the skill they need to achieve their goal. You can then work together to achieve ongoing success.

3 tips for clarifying the goals for a development session

"Agree on the goals when starting the session," is the golden rule. This sounds so obvious, much like 'teaching granny to suck eggs'. But it is a vital step in achieving success. Certainly I have hit trouble by wrongly assuming a person – or a group – wants to focus on certain issues. Fortunately it has been possible to recover by going back and making clear contracts about the agenda. Let's explore how to clarify the goals for a mentoring, coaching, team or other development session.

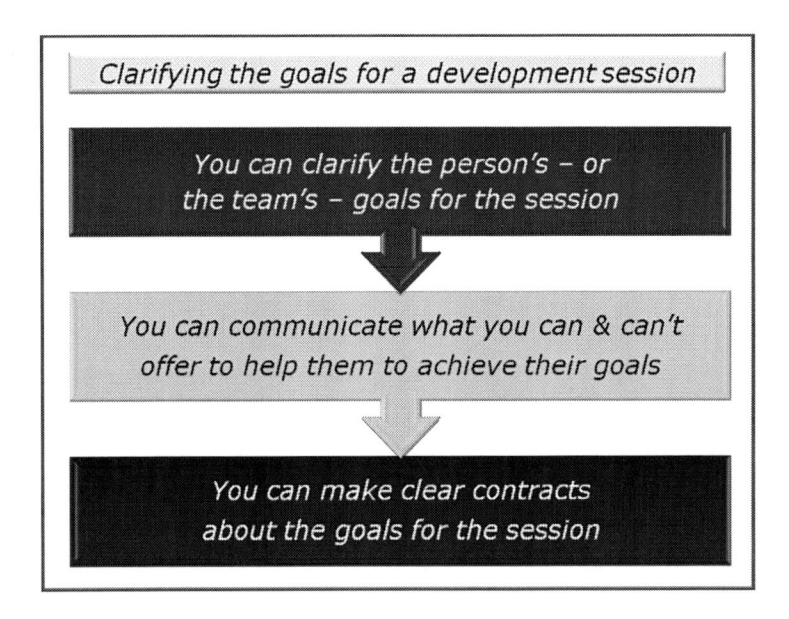

Clarifying the goals for a development session

- You can clarify the person's – or the team's – goals for the session
- You can communicate what you can & can't offer to help them to achieve their goals
- You can make clear contracts about the goals for the session

1) You can clarify the person's – or the team's – goals for the session.

"Normally I email a mentee one week before a session," said one person. "I invite them to let me know the kind of topics they want to

Sharing Knowledge

explore during the meeting. Sometimes they do not get round to replying, so I check their goals at the start of the session."

"I follow the same process when running a workshop, but in much greater detail. It is absolutely vital to be crystal clear on the goals ahead of time, otherwise you can get into deep trouble. So I always talk with the key person to ensure everybody wants to achieve the same aims. Agreeing the 'What' gives me time to prepare 'How' to reach their goals. Obviously I also re-contract at the start of the workshop to make sure everybody is still on the same page."

You will have your own methods for clarifying the goals for a coaching, mentoring or other development session. For example, you may ask the person or leader: "What are the topics that it would be useful to explore? What would you like to take away from the session? What for you would make it a successful session?" It sounds obvious, but 'knowing your destination is a vital part of the journey'. It's amazing how often this gets overlooked. Try completing the following sentence.

The specific things I can do to make sure that I clarify the person's – or the team's – specific goals for a session are:

* ....

* ....

* ....

2) You can communicate what you can & can't offer to help them to achieve their goals.

This is a vital step in clear contracting. Once the person – or the group – has said what they want, explain what you can and can't offer. You may say something like:

"I can provide practical tools that will help you to achieve goals a, b & c. Some of the other goals may require more specialist attention. If you would like to go-ahead, it would be good to clarify the respective roles. My responsibility to help you achieve the goals is to … The help I would like from you – or your team – is to … Providing we do these things, I am sure we have a good chance of reaching the goals. Would you like to go ahead?"

You will obviously communicate these messages in your own way. People often find it reassuring to know what you can and can't offer – rather than you claiming to offer every possible service. Try completing the following sentence.

The things I can do to communicate what I can and can't offer to help the person – or the team – to achieve their goals are:

* ....
* ....
* ....

3) You can make clear contracts about the goals for the session.

Conclude this part of the discussion by making clear contracts. It is good to recap 'What' you aim to achieve and 'How' you intend to work together. Bearing in mind what you have covered, you may say something like:

"Let's just recap on the goals for the session. You want to achieve a, b and c. My role in making this happen is ... Your role is ..."

You can then embark on the real work in the session. Try completing the following sentence.

The specific things I can do to finalise the contracts about what we will cover and the respective roles in the session are:

* ....
* ....
* ....

Contracting is crucial when you are providing a service. It's vital to take the time to be crystal clear on the goals for a session. This will provide the foundation for achieving success.

3 tips for understanding the picture inside someone's head

Great listeners listen for the 'theme' in what a person is saying. They then 'play back' the message to check they have understood the meaning. This is vital whether you are working as a coach, making clear contracts with a customer, listening to your partner or whatever. A key skill in this process is being able to see the world from the other person's point of view. Let's explore one approach to achieving this goal.

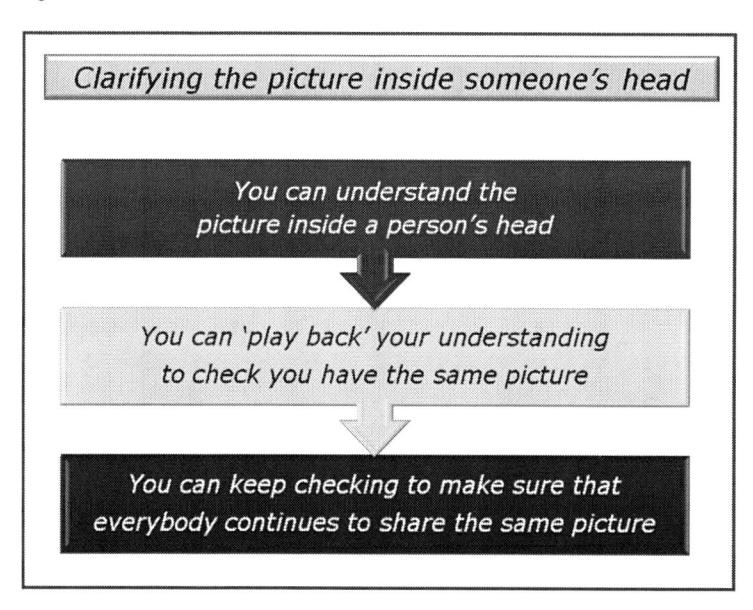

Clarifying the picture inside someone's head

You can understand the picture inside a person's head

⬇

You can 'play back' your understanding to check you have the same picture

⬇

You can keep checking to make sure that everybody continues to share the same picture

1) You can understand the picture inside a person's head.

Words can mean different things to different people. So it is vital to understand a situation from the other person's view. Here is an exercise that is used on workshops to illustrate how the same message can be interpreted in different ways. You ask the

The Strengths Toolbox

participants to close their eyes and then give the following instructions.

"Imagine a field in the country. In the field there is a horse. It is up to you what colour the horse is – brown, black, white or whatever. There may be other animals around. There might be a farmhouse or other buildings nearby. It is up to you what kind of day it is. The horse runs around the field, jumps over a fence and runs away into the distance. You can open your eyes now. Form pairs and each spend 30 seconds describing your picture."

Calling people together, you ask: "What colour was the horse?" People answer: "brown", "black", "white" or whatever. So you ask: "What is the right colour?" Blank stares. So you say:

"Every person's picture is right for them. You would think it was crazy if you saw a black horse and I said you got the wrong colour – it was white. But have you ever been in that situation? You think you have made an agreement with somebody. But then, when you follow up afterwards, they say you have got the wrong picture. Good communicators often finish a conversation by making clear contracts. They make sure everybody has agreed on the 'colour of the horse'."

Let's return to the art of listening to another person. Try tackling the exercise on this theme. First, think of a situation where you want to be a good listener – perhaps with your manager, with your partner or wherever. Second, describe the specific things that you can do to understand the 'picture inside their head' – the feeling they have, the situation from their point of view. Try completing the following sentences.

The specific situation where I want to be a good listener is:

* ....

The specific things I can do to understand the 'picture inside the person's head' are:

* ....

* ....

* ....

2) You can 'play back' your understanding to check you have the same picture.

Good communication calls for double-checking your understanding of the other person's view. For example:

- Imagine your boss says they want something done 'as quickly as possible'. Does this mean when you have finished your present task, when you have time or immediately? (They probably want it done yesterday!)

- Imagine a person says they want you to 'encourage' them. Do they mean to praise them all the time, give positive but realistic feedback or make suggestions about how they can improve?

- Imagine your partner says they want you to change your behaviour. Do you understand the actions they want you to stop – and what they want you to do instead in the future?

Let's return to the situation in which you want to be a good listener. Try completing the following sentence.

The specific things I can do to double-check I have understood the picture inside the person's head are:

* ....
* ....
* ....

3) You can keep checking to make sure that everyone continues to share the same picture.

Circumstances can change and so can seemingly agreed pictures. Sometimes people tell you about the changes; sometimes they don't. Sometimes people think they have communicated the changes; but they haven't. Good communicators develop the discipline of checking out that everybody still has the same picture.

The Strengths Toolbox

Imagine you have taken a brief from a difficult client who continually changes their mind. When presenting back the work to the client, you can position it by saying: "Before I show the work, let's just go back to the brief we agreed. If circumstances have changed, that is okay. But here is what we have done so far according to the brief." You can then build from a common understanding.

Let's return to the situation where you want to be a good listener. How can you stay connected, be aware of any changes and make sure everybody still has the same picture? Try completing the following sentence.

The specific things I can do to make sure that everybody continues to share the same picture are:

* ....

* ....

* ....

Clear communication is a key component of healthy relationships – be these with customers, colleagues, friends or family. One way to achieve this is by continuing to 'check out the colour of the horse'. You will then have the basis for continuing to build good relationships.

3 tips for employing the 'second empathy'

Great coaches have two kinds of empathy. The first empathy is with people's actual situation. The second empathy is with people's aspirations. Empathy is being able to see, feel and experience the world from another person's point of view. Great coaches enable motivated people to make the transition between their actual situation and their aspirations. Let's explore how to make this happen.

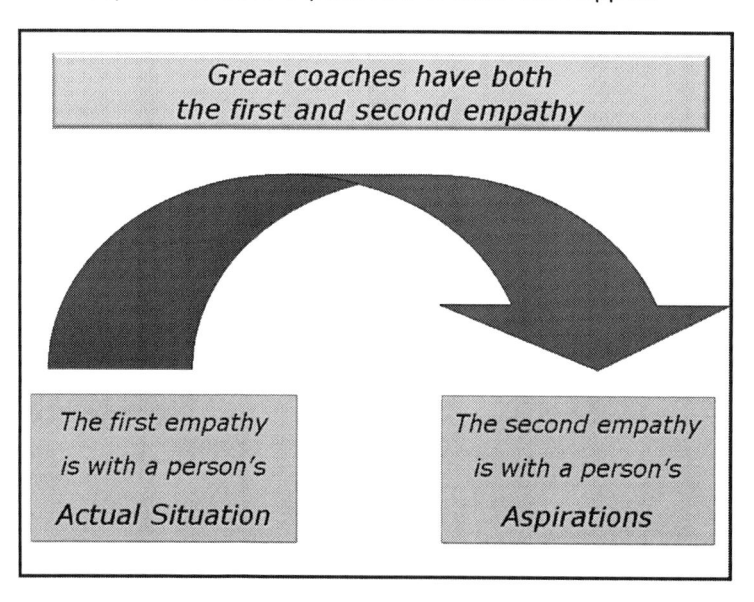

Great coaches have both the first and second empathy

The first empathy is with a person's Actual Situation

The second empathy is with a person's Aspirations

1) You can employ the first empathy and focus on the person's actual situation.

Imagine you are coaching somebody who has experienced a setback. The 'classical' approach is to spend considerable time showing the person you understand their situation. *But the key point is: for how long?* If you move on too quickly, they may feel you have not respected their feeling. If you linger too long, however, you give the problem too much power. Your aim is to enable a person to take control of their life – rather than to become a victim.

Great coaches may only need a few minutes to make a person feel welcome and tune into their world. They then encourage the person to choose whether: a) they want to dwell on their misfortune or; b) they want to direct their future. They accept the authenticity of the person's feelings. But then, when appropriate, begin helping them to explore their future options. So imagine you are coaching somebody who has experienced a setback. How can you connect with the person – but also be ready to help them to move forward? Try completing the following sentence.

The specific things I can do to demonstrate empathy with a person's actual situation are:

* ....

* ....

* ....

2) You can employ the second empathy and focus on the person's aspirations.

Somebody who has suffered a setback may need time in a sanctuary to lick their wounds. They can then emerge to shape their future and achieve success. You can work with them on:

- **Their short-term aspirations.**

People want to feel in control – so help them to 'control the controllables'. After suffering a setback – such as redundancy, loss or illness – resilient people take charge of their feelings, finances and future. Enable them to take charge of the 'practical things' – such as getting an income, getting a new job or whatever. But the key is to encourage them to take charge of the 'psychological things'. They can start by choosing their attitude – whether they are going to succeed or sulk. Then help them to explore their possible options – plus the consequences of each option – and pursue their chosen path. They can set short-term goals, translate these in action plans and get an early success. You can then move onto the next stage.

- **Their long-term aspirations.**

Good coaches encourage people to lift their sights to their overall picture of success. So you may invite the person to tackle exercises that clarify their life goals. Most people want similar things in life. They want to be loved, happy, creative, successful and find peace. Everybody will, of course, translate these into their own individual goals. People need hope – especially in the midst of chaos. Good coaches help people to clarify their long-term aims and choose their way forward. They also enable them to connect their short-term actions with their overall picture of success. This provides them with a sense of meaning.

So imagine you are coaching somebody who has experienced a setback. How can you connect with their short and long-term aspirations? Try completing the following sentence.

The specific things I can do to demonstrate empathy with a person's aspirations are:

* ....

* ....

* ....

3) You can help the person to fulfil their aspirations.

Good coaches recognise that: "Enlightenment is okay, but the hard part is execution." Many people have 'Ah yes,' moments, but then find it difficult to translate their visions into reality. If you are helping somebody who has suffered a setback, encourage them to 'take ownership' for shaping their future. Check they want: a) to move out of their sanctuary; b) to set specific goals; c) to work hard to achieve success. Encourage them to set short-term aims – because getting early wins builds confidence – and do something every day towards achieving their long-term aspirations. Try completing the following sentence.

The Strengths Toolbox

The specific things I can do to help a person to fulfil their aspirations are:

* ....

* ....

* ....

Good coaches are like great leaders – they keep moving between the 'concept' and the 'concrete'. Inspiring leaders reach people's hearts by saying things like: "We shall overcome ... I have a dream..." But they also show how to put the philosophy into practice. Good coaches embrace this ability and also demonstrate the two kinds of empathy. They connect with where the person is today. But then enable them to envisage and shape their tomorrow.

3 tips for using the three keywords 'what, how, when'

These were the three keywords I learned when working with young people in therapeutic communities. At the time there were many models for encouraging people, but most boiled down to asking them. "What do you want to do? How can you do it? When do you want to begin?" Let's explore how you can use these keywords to help people to succeed.

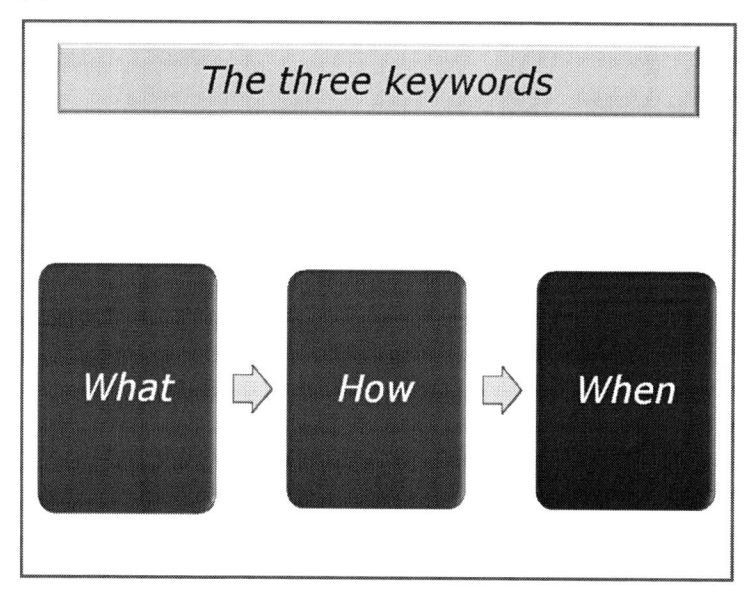

The three keywords

What ⇨ How ⇨ When

1) You can focus on the 'What'.

"Most people want similar things in life," said one of my early mentors in the therapeutic community. "They want to be loved, happy and successful. They also want to find peace. But people try to achieve these goals in different ways. Some strategies work, but others cause trouble. People who come to this community want to take responsibility for shaping their futures. We help them to clarify what they want out of life – then find healthy ways to achieve their goals."

Imagine somebody has asked you to help them to shape their future. You will probably start by clarifying their aims. Depending on the topic they want to explore, you will ask questions that revolve around the 'What'. For example:

"What is your goal? What are the real results you want to achieve? What is your picture of success?"

You may also use exercises to help a person clarify their short, medium and long-term goals. One of the most popular is called *Success.* Looking back when they are 80, what for them will mean they have had a successful life? If they prefer to simply focus on their professional life, they can tackle the exercise called *My professional legacy.* What do they want to leave behind after finishing a certain project or completing their career? There are many similar exercises that encourage people to clarify their 'What'.

"But what about the 'Why' question?" somebody may ask. "Don't they need to know why they want to achieve a goal?" I have found that people often find it easier to uncover their motives by asking them: "What will be the benefits of achieving the goal? What will be both the pluses and minuses? Bearing in mind the whole package, are you prepared to work hard to reach the goal?" In terms of deeper motives, I return to the key things that most people want out of life. They want to be loved, happy, successful and find peace. This means different things to different people. So quite a bit of time is spent on the question: "What are the *real results* you want to achieve?" Establish the 'What': then move onto the next step.

2) You can focus on the 'How'.

This is the opportunity to 'sit alongside' the person to do some brainstorming and creative problem-solving. When working with the young people, for example, I asked: "How can you get what you want?" This led to them exploring the specific actions – and successful patterns – they wanted to pursue in the future. Many had got themselves into trouble, so we also considered: "How can you stop yourself getting what you want?" This enabled them to describe their self-defeating patterns and the choices they could make.

Sharing Knowledge

Bringing it all together, the next question was: "So how can you do your best to reach your goals?" Let's imagine you have established the 'What' and the 'How' with the person, it is then time to move into action planning.

3) *You can focus on the 'When'.*

"When do you want to reach your goal? When do you want to pass the various milestones along the way? When can you get an early success? Bearing in mind these answers, when do you want to begin?" These are the key questions when enabling a person to clarifying their action plan. The crucial part, however, is that the person must 'own' the plan: they must believe in it and want to translate it into action. They must also be prepared to work hard to reach the goals. Before concluding a session, return to the beginning and double-check:

- The 'What' – the person's picture of success.
- The 'How' – the person's strategies for achieving success.
- The 'When' – the person's specific action plan for doing their best to achieve success.

The model sounds simple in theory – but you can practise it on many different levels. If you wish, try tackling the exercise at the end of this piece. Think of a specific situation where you would like to encourage a person. Then explore how you can use 'what, how, when' for helping them to reach their goals.

The specific situation in which I would like to use the three keywords for helping a person to achieve success is:

* ....

What. The specific things I can do to encourage the person to clarify their 'What' are:

* ....

* ....

* ....

How. The specific things I can do to encourage the person to clarify their 'How' are:

* ....

* ....

* ....

When. The specific things I can do to encourage the person to clarify their 'When' are:

* ....

* ....

* ....

3 tips for educating people by focusing on the 3 Is

Imagine you have been asked to educate a group of hungry students. How can you make the learning real, relevant and rewarding? Great educators often focus on the 3 I's: inspiration, implementation and integration. Let's explore how you can follow these steps to be a good educator.

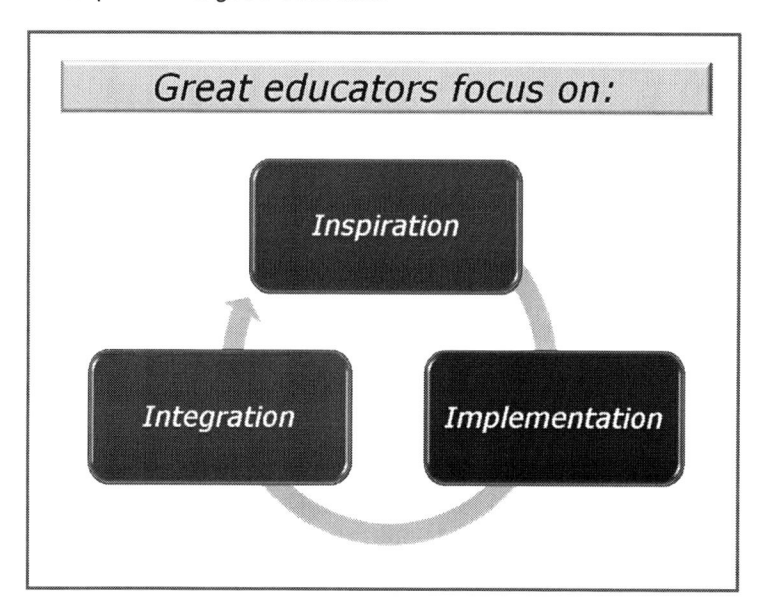

Great educators focus on:
- Inspiration
- Implementation
- Integration

1) You can focus on inspiration.

Great educators start by creating an inspiring environment in which motivated people can learn. For example, they show enthusiasm for their subject, link the learning to people's lives and make the sessions enjoyable and effective. They encourage, educate and enable people be successful in their lives and work. How can you inspire learners in your own way? If you are educating student teachers for example, you may want to start by inviting them to tackle an exercise called *My positive teacher*. Invite each person to look back on their life and describe a person who has helped them to learn. It may have been a parent, a teacher in school, a sports coach or whoever. What did that educator do right? How can they follow these principles to help others to learn? This kind of exercise involves both the heart and the head. There are many ways to create an inspiring environment and you will develop your own methods, so try completing the following sentence.

The things I can do to inspire people are:

* ....

* ....

* ....

2) You can focus on implementation.

Great educators provide implementation tools that work. They are able to go from the philosophical to the practical, from the conceptual to the concrete. They provide knowledge, models, and tools that people can use in their daily lives and work. How do they gather this information? Great educators frequently study success. They study the principles that people follow to reach their goals – then translate these into practical tools. The next stage is to invite people to test the tools in reality – just to make sure they work. If so, the tools are added to the repertoire of options that people can use to reach their goals. Try completing the following sentence.

The things I can do to provide implementation tools that work are:

* ....

* ....

* ....

3) You can focus on integration.

Great educators encourage people to integrate the learning in their own way. Why? People must 'own' the knowledge to apply it successfully – whether they are developing skills in computing, cookery, creativity, dancing, engineering, economics, football or whatever. How do you know when somebody has integrated an idea? They use their own language and methods to explain what they are doing and make things happen. Certainly they may follow 'eternal principles' – but they do so by using their own strengths and sometimes adding a touch of magic. Try completing the following sentence.

The things I can do to help people to integrate the learning in their own way are:

* ....

* ....

* ....

Different people are good at different aspects of the 3 Is. Some keynote speakers, for example, may score highly on inspiration. Some coaches score highly on implementation. Great educators get the right balance between inspiration, implementation and integration. They encourage, equip and enable their students to achieve ongoing success.

3 tips for running an enjoyable and effective educational session

Imagine you have been asked to run an educational session on, for example, developing leadership skills. How can you do a superb job? One approach is to follow the '1 – 2 – 3' model for running an enjoyable and effective session. Let's explore how this works in practice.

Running an educational session – the 1-2-3 model

Start the session. Win and inspire people in your own way.

1) Introduce the first theme.

- Give an introduction to the theme.
- Give examples from everyday life and work.
- Give models and tools.

2) Give an activity on the theme.

- Give an exercise that brings the learning to life.
- Give people chance to 'own' the knowledge.
- Give people chance to produce a finished 'product'.

3) Sum-up the theme – then link to the next theme.

- Give people chance to clarify their learning.
- Give more models and tools on the theme.
- Give a summary of the theme – then link to the next theme.

You will prepare properly before the session. For example, you will settle on the themes you want to cover, such as:

- Great leaders – giving an overview of what great leaders do right;
- Great leadership in your past experience – giving exercises where the participants learn from their own experiences of leadership;

- Great leadership in your work place – providing tools the participants can use to build on their strengths as leaders, etc.

Looking at how to bring these themes to life, you ask yourself: "What do I want people to learn? How can I help them to learn this in an enjoyable and effective way? When do I want to cover the various themes during the session?" Collecting these ideas together, you clarify the map for the session.

Let's move onto the actual session. Welcome people, establish credibility and inspire people in your own way. Describe the topics you will cover and what the participants will 'take away' from the session. Ensure this fits their agenda. Ask if there are any other topics they want to cover. Then follow the 1 – 2 – 3 model for running an enjoyable and effective educational session. Let's explore how to use this model in your own way.

1) You can introduce the first theme.

Give an introduction to the first theme. Give colourful examples that relate to people's daily work. If appropriate, you may then want to widen the topic. For example, invite people to identify what great leaders do right; share models about great leadership; show a clip of a great leader's speech or whatever. Great educators move from the 'concept' to the 'concrete', so link any models to daily work. Show that 'you know your stuff'. Begin giving some practical tools on the topic. Show the benefits of using these tools. Then move onto the next step.

2) You can give an activity on the theme.

Great educators know that people must 'own' the knowledge. So they often follow the 3I model – Inspiration, Implementation, Integration. They create an inspiring environment, provide implementation tools that work and help people to integrate the learning into their lives and work.

You can do this on a mini-scale during the session. Give people a relevant activity on the theme – some 'learning by doing' – such as an exercise or other learning experience. Make sure it is relevant and provides real 'take away' value. People obviously learn in different ways – so use different media. These might include giving input, using flip charts, using Power Points and giving the participants chance to clarify their own experiences. When giving people 'group work', make sure they must produce a 'finished product', such as a presentation. Then move onto the next step.

3) You can sum up the theme – then link to the next theme.

Summarise the key points. If appropriate, give more input – such as practical tools, models and know-how. Show how these can be applied in people's lives and work. Answer any questions and invite people to clarify their learning. Conclude your input on the theme – then link to the next theme. Repeat the '1 – 2 – 3' model until you have covered all the themes. After the session, clarify what you did well and what you can do better next time. Continue to develop as an educator.

3 tips for moving between the concept and the concrete

Imagine you are a mentor, educator or keynote speaker. How can you communicate in a way that people find relevant and rewarding? People often want to understand the overall philosophy but also get practical tools. One approach is to keep moving between the concept and the concrete. Let's explore how this works in practice.

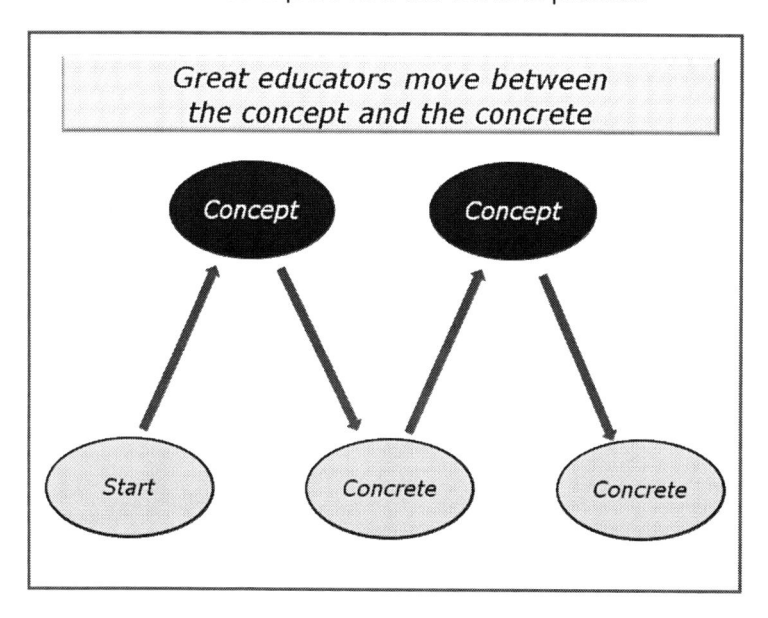

Great educators move between the concept and the concrete

Concept — Concept

Start — Concrete — Concrete

1) You can give the concept.

Imagine you are helping people to develop their leadership skills. Begin by clarifying the key messages you want to give people. Plan how you can bring these messages to life by moving between the concept and concrete. One message you may want to give, for example, is that the leader is always 'on stage'. Start by introducing the concept. You may want to say something like:

The Strengths Toolbox

"The leader is always 'on stage'. People will pick up on your mood. They will watch the way you communicate, speak and act. Looking back on your own life, remember how you reacted to parents, teachers and your managers. You probably watched them closely to 'read' their emotions – then judged what it was safe to say or do. Leaders set the tone – which is what you do in your daily work. Let's consider how to translate this principle into practice."

2) You can move to the concrete.

Show that you understand people's world by linking the concept to concrete actions. There are many ways to bring the learning to life. Here is a snapshot of one approach. You may want to say something like:

"Let's start from your destination and do three things. First, write the *actual words* you want people to say about you as a leader. For example: 'She/he is always positive. She/he communicates a clear vision. She/he always has time for us as individuals.' Second, describe your leadership journey during the working day – especially the interactions you have with employees. Third, describe how you want to behave during each part of this journey – especially when you are 'on stage'. Remember the impressions you want people to take away from their interactions with you.

"Let's start the journey. When do people see you for the first time during the day? Perhaps when you get out of the car; then you enter the building; greet the receptionist; enter the lift; say 'hello,' to others in the lift; walk into the main office; say 'hello,' to individuals; greet your PA; get yourself a coffee; talk with people at the coffee machine; walk back through the office; sit in front of the computer; begin work; answer the phone; walk around the office and so on. Looking at your journey, ask yourself:

- How do I want to behave when I meet each person? If a video camera followed me during the day, what would people see? What messages do I want to give? How can I give these in a positive but natural way?

Sharing Knowledge

- How do I want to greet people? How can I be fully present and give each person 100% attention? How can I show a sincere interest in them? What are the specific things I want to say to each person?

- What impression do I give when I walk through the office? Do I appear friendly, preoccupied or disinterested? What messages do I want to give? How can I do this in a natural way?

- What impression would people get of me if they saw me at my computer? Would it be better for me to have my own office – or be facing the wall – so that people do not read too much into my expressions?

- Everybody needs 'personal space' where they can just be themselves. What can I do to create this reflection time or space to relax? Once I have taken 'time out', how can I then refocus and go back into the situation where I am 'on stage'?"

Keep giving concrete examples. Answer questions and, where appropriate, give practical tools that people can use in their daily lives and work.

3) *You can keep moving between the concept and the concrete.*

Some teachers stay on the conceptual level; others stay on the concrete. Great educators move between the two levels. After covering the first topic, move onto the second and repeat the process. Try tackling the exercise on this theme. Looking ahead, think of a situation where you want to use this approach. First, describe the key messages – the concepts – you want to give people. Second, describe the examples you can use to bring these to life and make them concrete. When communicating, make sure that: a) You are connecting with people; b) You are helping them to reach their goals. People are then more likely to find the messages both relevant and rewarding. Try completing the following sentences.

Moving between the concept and the concrete

The first message. The concept I want to give is:

* ....

The practical examples and tools I can give to make this concrete are:

* ....

* ....

* ....

The second message. The concept I want to give is:

* ....

The practical examples and tools I can give to make this concrete are:

* ....

* ....

* ....

The third message. The concept I want to give is:

* ....

The practical examples and tools I can give to make this concrete are:

* ....

* ....

* ....

3 tips for communicating with 'architects', 'builders' and 'craftsmen'

Imagine you are due to make a presentation to a leadership team. The group will be made up of people who process information in different ways. There will be 'architects', 'builders' and 'craftsmen'. Let's consider these three types and how you can communicate with them successfully.

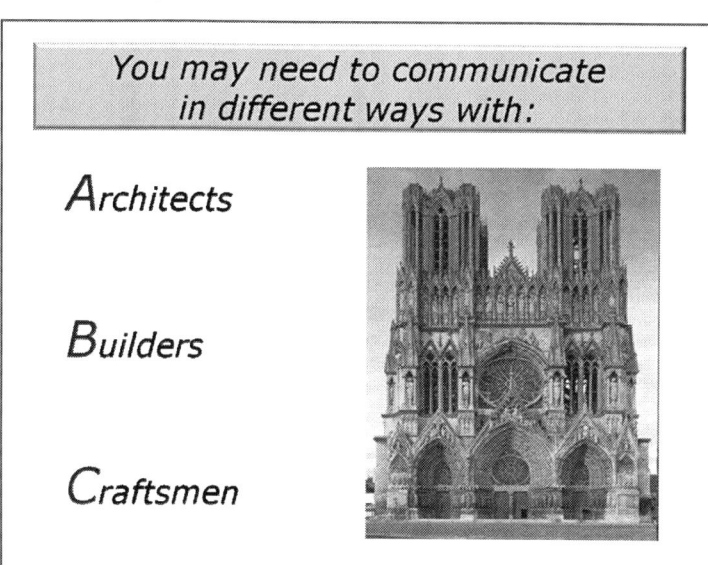

You may need to communicate in different ways with:

Architects

Builders

Craftsmen

1) Architects.

Architects are often decision makers and see the big picture. They like headlines. So quickly explain the results you aim to achieve – plus the benefits. They often go: 'a, b … then leap to … z'. Visionary by nature, they tend not to get into details, though they may ask the odd 'curve ball' question to check if you have done your homework. Providing you have a 'values fit' with them, they will want you to explain the broad principles you will follow to achieve the vision.

Architects sometimes have a short attention span – so double-check they are still on board – otherwise they may get bored and cause difficulties. Once onside, however, you will find they are great advocates. Try completing the following sentence.

The things I can do to communicate with 'architects' are:

* ....

* ....

* ....

2) *Builders.*

Builders pursue a more 'logical' thought process of going 'a, b, c, d, e …' until they get to 'z'. For example, they may be project managers who concentrate on the implementation plans. They focus on the processes to be followed to get the job done. So you must have your facts ready to answer their questions. If possible, meet with the key 'architects' and 'builders' before the presentation to agree on the principles for making things happen. You will need the builders onside if you want the 'building' – the project or other piece of work – to be finished. Try completing the following sentence.

The things I can do to communicate with 'builders' are:

* ....

* ....

* ....

3) *Craftsmen.*

Craftsmen are specialists who are often individual knowledge workers. Knowing every detail in their field, they are likely to discuss the intricacies of engraving each 'brick'. Sometime they can throw presentations off track by interrupting in mid-sentence, saying: "Do

Sharing Knowledge

you realize the problems involved in point 'c'?" Craftsmen care deeply about their work – so you need them onside. One approach is to provide them with a detailed compendium that gives answers to their key questions. You can refer to how their concerns are covered in the back-up material – then continue with the flow of your presentation. Try completing the following sentence.

The things I can do to communicate with 'craftsmen' are:

* ....
* ....
* ....

Presentations obviously work best when you prepare properly – so try to lay the groundwork. Before the session, start by getting the architects onside and, if possible, get one-to-one meetings with the builders and craftsmen. During these meetings you will, of course, need to present the information in different ways for people with different learning styles. Whenever possible, get everybody on board beforehand. This will give you the greatest chance of success.

3 tips for educating people to 'see' things in a professional situation

Peak performers 'see' things quickly in their area of brilliance. They have what is called 'personal radar'. Going into a situation, they quickly scan it to see patterns and then extrapolate those patterns. They seem to know 'what will happen before it happens.' Each person has good radar in specific areas but bad radar in others. So is it possible to help somebody to see things more quickly, more deeply and improve their radar? Providing they have some 'feeling' for the activity, the answer is 'Yes'. Let's explore how to make this happen.

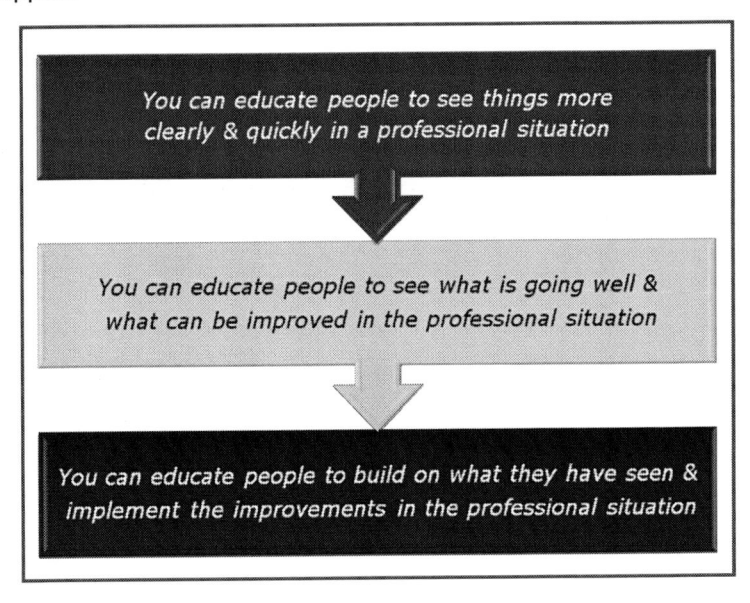

You can educate people to see things more clearly & quickly in a professional situation

↓

You can educate people to see what is going well & what can be improved in the professional situation

↓

You can educate people to build on what they have seen & implement the improvements in the professional situation

1) *You can educate people to see things more clearly & quickly in a professional situation.*

People with good radar quickly get to the heart of a matter. They 'see' and 'sense' things more deeply and quickly than others. The

Sharing Knowledge

superb sales person senses how to close a deal; the great footballer spots the opportunity for a defence splitting pass; the wise mediator recognises the opportunity to find a 'win-win' solution. Some radar is given – it is a gift with which we are born. But it can be developed through education and experience. How to make this happen? One approach is to 'physically take people through the journey' and clarify what they actually see in a professional situation.

Let me illustrate this approach by describing an exercise involving the staff from a high tech company. (You can apply the same principles to any kind of professional situation.) A key customer had recently complained that the company's building looked shoddy, saying: "I hope the staff members take more care of their software than they do of the building." This sparked some debate. But the outcome was that the leader asked me to 'educate' the staff about improving the experience for visiting customers. We agreed to start with a task force of volunteers who were committed to making improvements.

I asked the people in the task force to meet me at 8.30 in the morning. Not in the office, but half a mile further away, on the main road that led to the company headquarters. Gathering the group together, I gave the instructions.

"We are going to walk towards the office. The customers would be coming in their cars – so I want you to see the journey through their eyes. You each have 3 different coloured bundles of Post-it Notes. As we approach and then go into the office, I want you to write on the Post-It Notes.

- On the **Green** Post-its, write every positive impression you get about the company or good thing you see as a customer.
- On the **Red** Post-its, write every negative impression you get or thing that needs to be fixed.
- On the **Blue** Post-its, write every idea you have for what could be done to improve the customer's experience.

"Write one idea per Post-it. We will theme these at the end, consider the ideas and then implement the actions. Fine, let's begin walking towards the building."

The Strengths Toolbox

How can you apply this approach in your own way? Begin by describing a situation where you would like to make it happen. Try completing the following sentence.

The specific situation where I want to educate people to see things more clearly and quickly is:

* ....

2) You can educate people to see what is going well and what can be improved in the professional situation.

The team set off at speed. Within 20 metres I said, "Stop. Wait a minute. Remember you are a customer travelling in a car towards the company. What do you see? Can you see the sign directing you to the company? What are your first impressions?"

"There is a sign when you get near the gate," said one person, "but not one here. Sometimes we get complaints about people overshooting the drive. But we do send them a map."

People started scribbling on the Post-its. We continued the walk. On our left were railings and a hedge – through which we could see the building. So I asked people to stop again and describe what they saw. They mentioned the railings – but not the beer cans that lay at the bottom of the hedge. "But we can't do anything about that," said one person. "It's the problem of being on a main road." More scribbling on the Post-its.

Passing the unsmiling security guard, we approached the main building. Standing on the steps were 3 staff members smoking their last cigarettes before going into work. Not the best first impression to give a visiting customer planning to give a cheque to the company. So we went on. The journey took us past the into the shabby reception area, to the toilet, onto the coffee area and so on. Sixty minutes later the task force had compiled masses of Post-it Notes. The majority were red and blue.

This is a simple but powerful exercise. I have used it in many situations – with hotel staff, footballers, therapists and other professionals. The aim is to get people to take time to, identify what they 'see' – then focus on what can be improved. It is to increase their awareness and expand their radar. How can you apply this approach in your own way? Try completing the following sentence.

The specific things I can do to educate people to see what is going well and what can be improved in the professional situation are:

* ....

* ....

* ....

3) You can educate people to build on what they have seen & implement the improvements in the professional situation.

"Some things we had simply stopped seeing," said one person. "Other things we would never have thought of until today – such as the idea of putting fruit in the reception for customers."

The task force arranged the Post-its in their respective colours – then sorted these into themes. Within two hours they had produced a comprehensive action plan – complete with getting some early successes, such as clearing of hedges each day. One person remarked: "We can improve things straight away – and most of the improvements cost very little money." The big challenge would be for them to keep 'seeing' what could be improved.

You can use this approach in your own way, but bear in mind the concept of 'personal radar'. Some people will see things more quickly and more deeply than others in particular activities – but they may not 'see' anything in other places. Providing people do have some feeling for an activity, however, you can educate them to keep improving their vision. Try completing the following sentence.

The Strengths Toolbox

The specific things I can do to educate people to build on what they have seen and implement improvements in the professional situation are:

* ....

* ....

* ....

3 tips for understanding change on the primary and secondary levels

Imagine you are a leader, manager or coach who has been charged with: "Helping people to transform their behaviour." Several things will be important to remember. First, to establish their 'will' before imparting any skill – people must want to develop. Second, to understand the primary and secondary levels of learning. (See below.) Third, to encourage people to get some early wins. Finally, to help them to understand how to follow the successful principles in the future. Let's explore how people can develop on both the primary and secondary levels – because both are crucial if they are to achieve success.

People learn on both the primary & secondary levels

Secondary Level	Talking	Intellectualising	Thinking
Primary Level	Doing	Playing	Feeling

1) The primary level.

People learn on two levels: the primary level and the secondary level. When we are children, we start by learning on the primary level. This is the level of doing, playing and feeling. We adventure, explore and gather experience. Living on the primary level is great, but we must make sense of experience, which leads to the next stage.

2) *The secondary level.*

People also learn on a secondary level – which is vital for creating models and frameworks for understanding our experience. Learning from the past, we translate these lessons into actions for the future.

But sometimes people hit a problem. They spend too much of their lives on the secondary level. Instead of doing, they think about doing. Instead of 'playing' – taking initiatives – they replace it with intellectualising. Instead of feeling, they talk about feelings. Between the two levels they then put a series of blocks. This creates differences between 'what they say and what they do'. Companies also fall into this trap. For example, they may issue a finely worded 'values statements', but this is purely secondary level. They don't live the values.

3) *Change on the primary and secondary levels.*

Learning takes place on both levels – *but real growth begins on the primary level.* People must *do* something that brings success. They take this step by either: a) Doing things they already know work; or b) Doing new things that work. They feel better, get better results or build better relationships. Success breeds success. They integrate the habits and change their behaviour. These patterns become integrated and part of their 'default'. Let's explore how it works in practice.

Therapists can help a client to analyse 'why' they have problems – but the 'talking cure' has limits. People who retake control of their lives do so *by acting on the primary level.* They do something physical. They start running; stay sober rather than drink; or spend time with positive rather than negative people. Individuals who develop good habits are more likely to feel successful.

Companies that aim to shift their culture must start on the primary level. "Never lead with a piece of paper," is the mantra. They must *do* something different. Leaders can talk till they are blue in the face – but people will be watching their behaviour. They must change the physical things to change the psychological things to change the philosophical things. Companies that do this stand a chance of shifting their culture.

People may be successful on the primary level – but they must know how to repeat the principles. This calls for developing an understanding on the secondary level. They need a model, framework or tool they can use to repeat the success.

So how can you help people to transform their behaviour? First, establish their 'will'. Are they serious? Bearing in mind the pluses and minuses involved, do they accept the whole package? Second, encourage them to do what works on the primary level. Third, help them to get some early wins. Finally, enable them to understand and repeat the key principles. People will then stand a good chance of achieving ongoing success.

3 tips for producing great design

Imagine you have been asked to design something. It could be a workshop, garden, house, furniture, solution, article or whatever. "Great design is simple, satisfying and successful," we are told. Sounds simple in theory, but it can be hard to achieve in practice. Let's explore how you can follow these steps for producing great design.

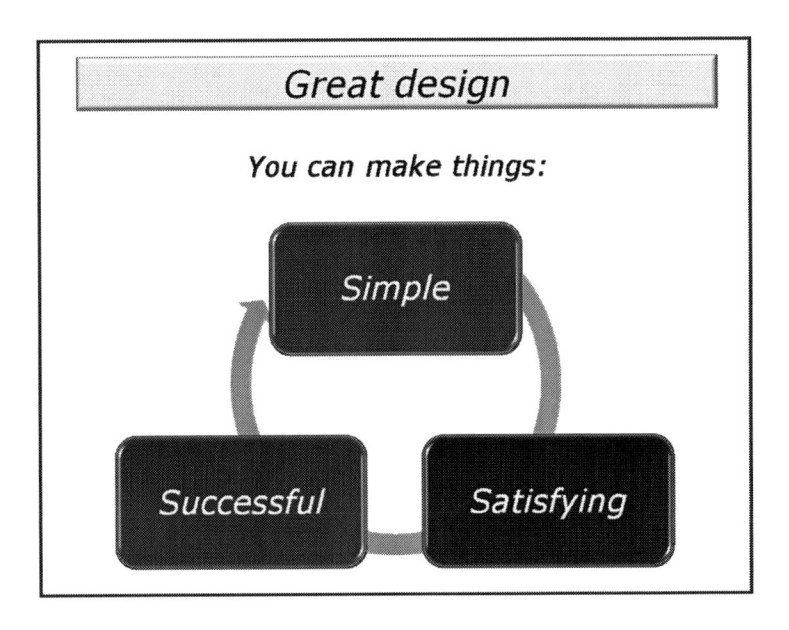

Great design

You can make things:

- Simple
- Successful
- Satisfying

1) You can make it simple.

Great teachers make complicated things simple – and so do fine designers. They produce things that are simple, beautiful and effective. Before embarking on your own design project, however, try clarifying your philosophy of design. Different people have different tastes, so think a design that you admire. You make like the original Sony Walkman, the Apple Mac or some other elegant solution. What are the characteristics of the design you admire? Try completing the following sentences.

Sharing Knowledge

The piece of design that I admire is:

* ....

The specific things I admire about this piece of design are:

* ....

* ....

* ....

Let's move onto the specific thing you want to create – be it a garden, an article, a tool or whatever. Designers begin by asking themselves questions such as:

"What are the real results I want to achieve? Who is the target group who will be using the design? What do they want it to achieve? What are the resources available? What information do I need? How can I gather this information – then boil it down to its essence? How can I design something that works? How can I test it out? How can I improve the design? How can I make it as simple as possible?"

The final point is crucial. William Strunk and E.B.White produced the writer's bible *The Elements of Style,* which still used widely today. The book urged writers to 'keep it simple'. It also included rules such as: 'Choose a suitable design and hold to it … Put statements in a positive form … Use definite, specific, concrete language … Omit needless words … Place the emphatic words of a sentence at the end." Great design is simple, but not 'simplistic'. Like great teaching, it often contains a 'profound simplicity'.

Let's return to the thing you want to produce. How can you clarify the results you want to achieve? How can you collect information? How can you boil it down to its essence? Try completing the following sentence.

The specific things I can to do to make the design simple are:

* ....

* ....

* ....

The Strengths Toolbox

2) You can make it satisfying.

Great design is satisfying on a number of levels. Physically – it looks and feels good: practically – it works and is user-friendly; psychologically – it is aesthetically and sensually pleasing. Herman Miller's famous Aeron chair, for example, embodies many of these elements. The website http://www.designfeast.com provides a massive repertoire of tools, knowledge and ideas that people can use. It also offers an array of quotes on the topic. Here is a selection.

"Design is art that makes itself useful."
1984 poster for Die Neue Sammlung, design museum, Munich

"Don't make something unless it is both necessary and useful; but if it is both necessary and useful, don't hesitate to make it beautiful."
Shaker lesson

"One of the main criteria for the design of the everyday, though, is sensuality. Something that is sensual evokes a response that's not just visual or intellectual: It's suggestive."
Deborah Berke, Principal, Deborah Berke Architect PC

Let's return to the piece you want to produce. How can you make it satisfying on different levels? Try completing the following sentence.

The specific things I can to do to make the design satisfying are:

* ....

* ....

* ....

3) You can make it successful.

Great design works. It does the job. The Amazon web site made it easy for customers to buy books with 'one click'. First Direct made it easy for people to manage their banking. Terence Conran said: "Good design is probably 98% common sense. Above all, an object must function well and efficiently – and getting that part right requires a good deal of time and attention." Human beings are designers by nature. They love to follow the process of design, development and deliver. Looking at what you want to produce, try completing the following sentence.

The specific things I can to do to make the design successful are:

* ....

* ....

* ....

Human beings still face many design challenges. Perhaps the most urgent is to build a 'win-win' world. This will be one where every person has the physical and psychological opportunities to fulfil their talents. They will then be able to say: "Life has been great. I have done what I was meant to do on Earth." This calls for adding sustainability to the other design elements. People can continue to add to this spirit by creating things that are simple, satisfying and successful.

3 tips for understanding the 'second simplicity'

Wise people often demonstrate 'the second simplicity'. They get to the heart of the matter and say things that are 'simple' yet profound. Let's explore how people may get to this stage go through the years of simplicity, complexity – then onto the profound simplicity.

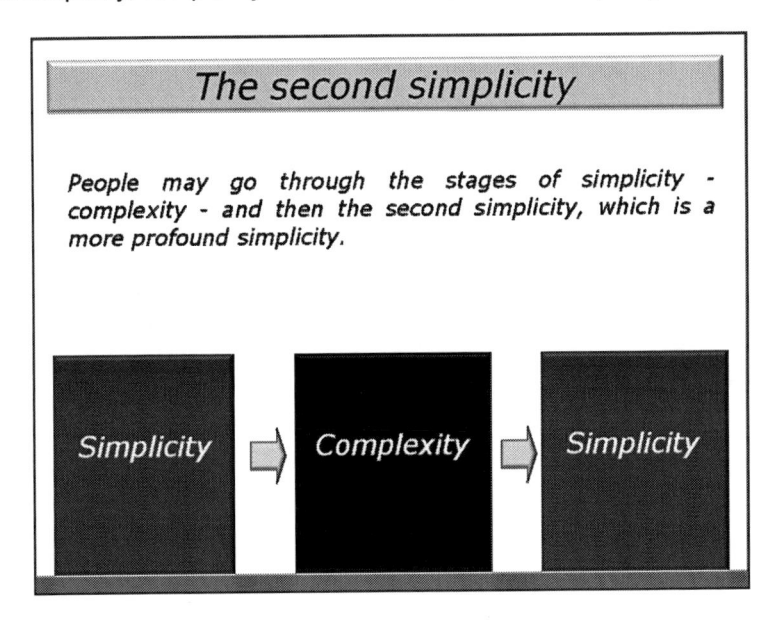

The second simplicity

People may go through the stages of simplicity - complexity - and then the second simplicity, which is a more profound simplicity.

Simplicity ⇨ *Complexity* ⇨ *Simplicity*

1) Simplicity.

"Life appeared simple when I was young," said one person. "As a teenager I believed in love, peace, beauty and building a better world. Powered by idealism, I threw myself into voluntary work, protested against racism and studied the great philosophies. Many thinkers reinforced my beliefs. There seemed obvious answers to solving the world's problems. My ideals kept me going into my early twenties."

Sharing Knowledge

What did you believe in during the years of your first simplicity? What were your dreams? What were your ideals? Try completing the following sentence.

The things I believed in during the years of my first simplicity were:

* ....
* ....
* ....

2) Complexity.

Then comes complexity. People go to work, enter university, graduate into the professions, become 'experts', speak in strange languages, write in long sentences, join big companies, get lost in matrix organisations, get married, incur debts, suffer setbacks, make compromises, bury their dreams and say "Life is not that simple."

Not everybody dives into complexity – but it can be tempting. For example, an older staff member gave me a tough message soon after I started working in a therapeutic community. I wrote a detailed report that was full of analysis about one of the 'patients'. Showing it to the staff member, I expected him to compliment me on the report. His response was:

"Your intention is good, but I can't understand your message. You seem to have swallowed a psychiatric dictionary. It is vital to go deep – but write your recommendations in words that people can understand. We are human beings who are trying to help other human beings."

Different people experience different 'wake up calls'. Those who are faced by life-threatening illnesses, for example, quickly reassess their priorities. They rise above the daily habits and focus on what is really important in life. Have you experienced such years of complexity? If so, try completing the following sentence.

The things that happened during the years of complexity were:

* ....

* ....

* ....

3) *Simplicity.*

The 'second simplicity' is a profound simplicity. A person may return to their original philosophy – but experience brings wisdom. The pains and pleasures of life add an extra timbre to their voice. Speaking from the depths of their being, their words resonate more deeply. They are 'real', rather than in 'role'. Making sense of their experience, they make complicated things simple. Embracing a sense of humility yet urgency, they share lessons from the second simplicity. They have wisdom in their bones. They pass on what they have learned in life. Try completing the following sentence

The things I believe in – or think I will believe in – during the years of my second simplicity are:

* ....

* ....

* ....

Sharing Knowledge

3 tips for finding 'win-win' solutions

Imagine you have been asked to find positive solutions to difficulties between people. You may have been invited to solve deep-seated conflicts, ongoing arguments or fundamental differences. Such situations are often the result of long-term patterns, so there is not a quick fix. The best route is to go for a 'win-win' solution, but this takes creativity and patience. 'Win-lose' creates ongoing problems; whilst 'lose-lose' spells trouble for everybody.

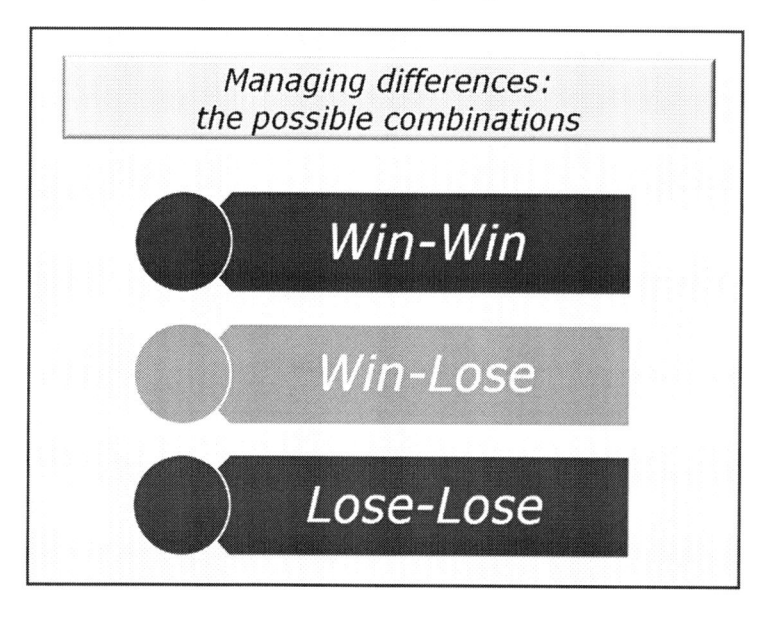

Managing differences: the possible combinations

- Win-Win
- Win-Lose
- Lose-Lose

Looks simple on paper – but we know it is extremely difficult in practice. Let's explore three steps towards making it happen.

1) You can make sure the conditions are in place for finding a 'win-win' solution.

Two conditions must be in place before it is possible to solve deep differences.

a) People must want to solve the conflict.
b) People must be prepared to work hard to – as far as possible – find 'win-wins'.

Timing is everything. Many conflicts only get resolved when the parties are exhausted. For example, couples feel wary from fighting a divorce, terrorists became too old or tired to fight, employers and strikers are exhausted after an industrial dispute. People get fed up with the negative energy. They are then more willing to sit down and find positive solutions. Before getting involved in any conflict resolution, it is important to ask the following questions:

- Are people ready to work together? Do they really want to solve the problem? (Remember, some people are addicted to conflict.)

- Are they prepared to co-operate to find – as far as possible – a 'win-win' solution? How high is their motivation to do this on a scale 0 – 10? (7+ is necessary to produce success.)

- Are people ready to focus on how things can be better in the future, rather than simply argue about the past?

Providing people want to solve the problem, it is then possible to move onto the next step.

2) You can clarify what each party wants and build on common ground – before then going onto the differences.

Start by clarifying what each person or party wants. Focus on what people have in common – rather than the differences. Some may try to draw you into arguing about the differences, but return to the similarities. You will have lots of time later to explore the differences. Mediators, for example, create a safe environment in which people feel at ease. They listen to what each person perceives as the challenge. They then aim to build a common agenda. Doing this calls for following certain rules. It is important:

Sharing Knowledge

a) To show respect and recognise the authenticity of each person's feelings. Everybody must feel that they have been heard.
b) To encourage people to look to the future, rather than fight about the past.
c) To get people to be super specific about the desired outcome. Ask people: "What are the real results you want to achieve?"
d) To encourage the parties to put the challenge in positive terms. For example: "How can the two departments work together to achieve success?" Rather than: "How can they stop fighting?"
e) To build on the common ground, get some quick success and begin to build confidence.

You can use the following framework to map out what people want, what they have in common and the potential differences.

Party 'A' wants:

* ....

* ....

* ....

Party 'B' wants:

* ....

* ....

* ....

*The **common ground**. The common goals – the real results – that everybody wants to achieve are:*

* ....

* ....

* ....

*The **differences**. The potential different things that people want are:*

* ....

* ....

* ....

The things we can do to build on the common ground and get some quick successes are:

* ....

* ....

* ....

Build on what people have in common. Get some early successes, create confidence and build trust. Then go onto the next step.

3) You can then keep working until you find – as far as possible – 'win-win' solutions.

You can now move onto the differences. Start by establishing clarity. Looking at each difference in turn, clarify what each person/party wants. Then use the 5 C model for creative problem-solving. Focus on the challenges, choices, consequences, creative solutions and conclusions. (You can find an adaptation of this in the piece called *3 tips for facilitating a mentoring session*.) Stay calm and invite people to use their creativity. When it comes to the sticking points, keep asking:

How can we find a 'win-win' solution?

Sharing Knowledge

Be patient. People are incredibly creative – so keep asking this question until they solve the problem. (If appropriate, you can share possible ideas, but it is vital to show that you respect each person's agenda.) If tempers rise, take a break and have a cooling off period. Return to the beginning and establish if people still want to solve the problem. If so, resume the exploration. Keep going until they find, as far as possible, a 'win-win' solution. Again, build on the good work by getting an early success. Encourage people: a) To set clear goals; b) To make clear contracts about each person's contribution; c) To get a concrete result. Success breeds success and mutual confidence. People can then move onto the next topic where they want to find a 'win-win' solution.

Let return to the situation where you may have be asked to help with a difficult situation. Focus on one specific difference and try completing the following sentences.

The specific topic where people have differences is:

* ....

The specific things that party 'A' wants are:

* ....

The specific things that party 'B' wants are:

* ....

The potential options that could be – as far as possible – a 'win-win' solution are:

* ....
* ....
* ....

Sounds easy in theory – but it is obviously much harder in daily life. So how do painful problems get solved? There are several answers. Some don't – people go on fighting. Some do because people lose

The Strengths Toolbox

interest – they get tired, accept the differences or move on with their lives. Some do because people work hard at solving the problem. You can focus on situations that fall into the latter category. Equipping people to find 'win-win' solutions can provide them with a tool for life.

3 tips for running a super teams workshop

Imagine you are running a super teams workshop. You have already had a pre-meeting with the leader in which you both agreed on the goals for team session. The leader has also created their provisional picture of perfection. During the workshop you will provide practical tools that people can use:

- To set up the team to succeed.
- To agree on the team's picture of perfection.
- To agree on each person's contribution to achieving the picture of perfection.

Here are three steps you can take when running the actual workshop.

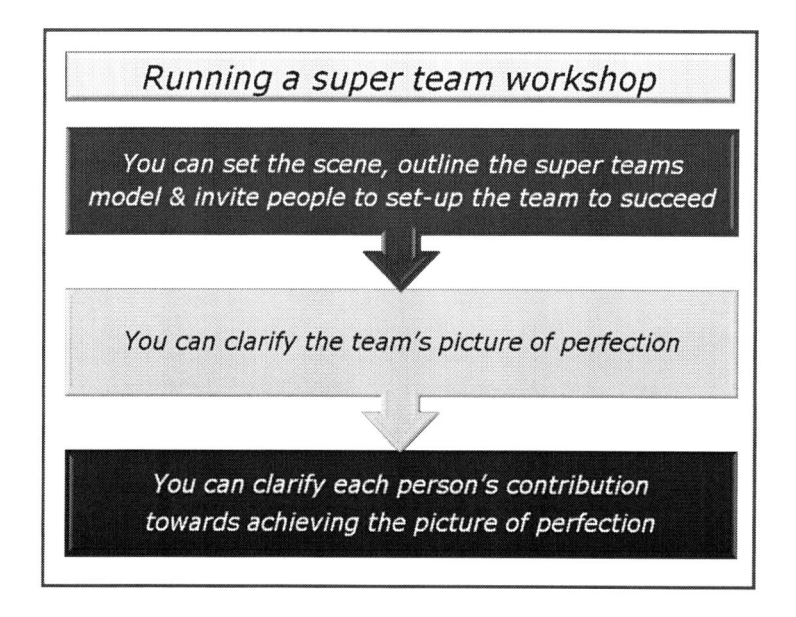

Running a super team workshop

You can set the scene, outline the super teams model & invite people to set-up the team to succeed

⬇

You can clarify the team's picture of perfection

⬇

You can clarify each person's contribution towards achieving the picture of perfection

The Strengths Toolbox

1) You can set the scene, outline the super teams model and invite people to set up the team to succeed.

- **Welcome people.**

Get the basics right. Ensure people are greeted properly. Provide them with coffee, tea, fruit or whatever. Make sure all the 'hygiene factors' are taken care of successfully.

- **Start the workshop.**

Invite the leader to kick off the session. They can give the background the workshop – the reasons for meeting today – and outline the goals. The leader then hands over to you.

- **Establish credibility and set the scene.**

Establish credibility in your own way. Different people have different ways of demonstrating they know their subject. Follow the style that works for you. Repeat the goals for the workshop. Give an overview of the day. For example, here is a possible schedule.

9.00 Start: introduction and goals for the workshop.

* *Super teams: an overview*
* *Setting up the team to succeed.*
* *Creating the right conditions for achieving success.*

Lunch

* *Clarifying the picture of perfection.*
* *Clarifying each person's contribution towards achieving the picture of perfection.*
* *Continuing to build a super team.*

17.00 Close.

Make clear working contracts. Explain what you see as: a) your role during the day, and b) The team's role during the day.

Sharing Knowledge

- **Give a brief introduction to super teams.**

Do this in a way that fits for you. For example, I often start by saying that super teams have several characteristics:

* They have a compelling 'story', a clear strategy and people combine their strengths to achieve success.
* They have 'similarity of spirit and diversity of strengths'.
* They make clear contracts. Contracting is crucial when working together to achieve the picture of perfection.

- **Give an activity in which people clarify some of the elements that make up a super team.**

People need an opportunity to 'own' the learning. So invite them to tackle the exercise called *Super teams.* Each person is to identify a team they have admired and what they did right to perform brilliant work. They are also to make a flip chart describing their example and put these around the room. People then form trios and share their findings. Bring the group back together. Invite two or three people to give a short summary of what their chosen team did well. Write these principles on a flip chart. You can then keep referring back to these themes during the workshop.

- **Give further input on building a Super Team.**

Go through the super teams model. In your own words, you may want to say something like: "There are many ways to climb a mountain. Similarly, there are many ways to build a great team. Here is one approach we will be looking at today." Talk through those parts of the model that you feel are relevant. Give real life examples that illustrate each theme.

- **Invite people to create the foundations for setting up the team to succeed.**

Ask people to tackle a series of exercises under the following headings.

a) People – the spirit we want in the team.
They are to do two things. First, to brainstorm and then agree on the characteristics – the spirit and qualities – they want people in the team to demonstrate. For example: to take responsibility; to

be positive; to be professional; to be customer-focused; to deliver. Second, to give *specific examples* of how each of these qualities would be demonstrated by people in the team.

b) Satisfying sponsors.

They are to do three things. First, to make a list of the 'sponsors' – the people who can hire or fire them – who they must continue to satisfy. Second, to describe the specific results they believe each of these sponsors wants delivered. Third, to describe the specific things they can do to satisfy these sponsors.

c) Controlling the controllables.

They are to do three things. First, to describe the specific things they as individuals and as a team can control. For example, their attitude, professionalism, etc. Second, to describe the things they can't control. For example, their bosses, the market, etc. Third, to describe how they can build on what they can control and manage what they can't control.

d) Super team contract.

They are to do two things. First, to describe what they see as the leader's responsibility in the team. Second, to describe what they see as the team members' responsibility in the team. This can then become the basis for their working contract.

e) Quick successes

They are to do three things. First, to describe the potential quick successes the team could achieve. Second, to give a probability rating of being able to deliver each of these successes. This to be done on a scale 0 – 10. Third, to describe the specific things that can be done to improve these ratings.

Prepare flip charts for each exercise ahead of time and put the flip charts on the floor. Ask people to go and stand on the topic they want to tackle and, in this way, form small groups. (You are reinforcing the voluntary principle.) People have 30 minutes to complete the exercise, including writing up the flip chart, before returning to the whole group. Each team then makes a 5-10 minute presentation. Frequently this leads to discussion. (By now it is probably time for lunch.)

Sharing Knowledge

Why introduce such exercises before exploring the picture of perfection? People will already have a rough idea of the goals. From a learning point of view, however, it is good to encourage participants to be active, rather than passive. People must also gain a sense of ownership in creating the foundations for the team. You will soon move onto the POP.

2) You can clarify the team's picture of perfection.

You can help the team to do this in two stages: a) The leader presents the picture of perfection; b) The team members then get a chance to add to the POP. Let's look at these stages.

- **Invite the leader to present the picture of perfection.**

The leader presents the road map towards achieving the picture of perfection. They can then describe the benefits and key strategies for achieving the goals. People can ask questions for information. They will later get a chance to add to the POP.

	The picture of perfection	
	The goal is:	
	To _____	
The date is:	The specific things we will have achieved by then will be:	The words we want to hear people saying then will be:
* _____	* _____	* _____
	* _____	* _____
	* _____	* _____
* _____	* _____	* _____
	* _____	* _____
	* _____	* _____
* _____	* _____	* _____
	* _____	* _____
	* _____	* _____

The Strengths Toolbox

- **Invite people to add to the POP.**

Before the workshop the main elements of the road map will have been transferred to flip charts. You can now 'roll out' the road map in front of the team. Give each person a pack of Post-It Notes. They have 10 minutes to write things they would like to see added to the POP. They are to write one idea per Post-It, but compile as many ideas as they wish. Each person then goes up in turn and puts their suggestions on the relevant parts of the road map. They are also to explain what they have written on each Post-It. The leader can take away the suggestions and consolidate the road map. They have the final say, of course, but it is good to incorporate many of the ideas into the road map.

Please note. Depending on the make-up of the overall team, you now have two options:

a) You may be running the workshop for a relatively small team. If so, invite people to clarify their individual contributions to the POP. (See later in this piece.)

b) You may be running a workshop for a big team, however, in which there are 'teams within the team'. If so, invite people to go into their natural teams. They are to produce their team's 'Road map towards achieving the picture of perfection.' They should then present this back to the big group, showing how their road map feeds into the overall POP. People can then complete the individual contribution exercise within their natural teams – perhaps a week a so after the workshop.

Let's imagine, however, that you are working with a team of individual contributors. You can then go onto the next step.

3) You can clarify each person's contribution towards achieving the picture of perfection.

- **Invite people to clarify and present their best contribution towards achieving the goals.**

Super teams encourage people to build on their strengths. So invite people to consider the activities in which they deliver 'As', rather than 'Bs' or 'Cs'. Bearing in mind their strengths, invite each person to tackle the exercise called *My contribution to the picture of perfection*.

My contribution to the picture of perfection

The goals. The specific results I aim to deliver are:

- _____
- _____
- _____

The benefits. The contribution this will make towards achieving the picture of perfection is:

- _____
- _____
- _____

The Strengths Toolbox

> **The style. The way I work best is:**
>
> - _____
> - _____
> - _____
>
> **The support. The support I would like is:**
>
> - _____
> - _____
> - _____
>
> **The measures. The specific things that will show I have reached the goals will be:**
>
> - _____
> - _____
> - _____

Give them 45 minutes to complete this work. Each person is then to make a 10 minutes presentation to the whole team about their contribution. Everybody then knows what mountain they are climbing, why they are climbing it and everybody's part in reaching the summit. The leader can meet with each person after the workshop to make clear contracts about their part in achieving the picture of perfection.

- **Invite people to clarify their 'take away' from the day.**

It is now time to wrap up the workshop. One approach is to ask people to clarify *Three things I have learned – or relearned – today*. Give individuals a few minutes to write these down by themselves, then to briefly share them, either in pairs or in the whole group. Doing such an exercise gives people a feeling of success. Thank people for their contribution to the workshop.

Sharing Knowledge

- **Invite the leader to conclude the session. They can describe how they want to maintain the momentum and continue building the super team.**

Keep close to the leader during the day and make sure they are happy that things are on track. During these discussions, invite them to consider how to maintain the momentum after the workshop. For example, getting the 'teams within the team' to report back within two weeks. They can report the progress they have made – including how they have got some early successes.

Ask the leader to close the workshop. They need to focus on: a) Their plans for meeting individuals to finalise each person's best contribution to the goals. b) Their plans for maintaining the momentum. This is not a one-off – people will be asked to keep updating the whole team on their contribution to the picture of perfection. c) Their plans for getting some quick successes. Finally, they can thank everybody for their contribution to the session.

This is one way to run a super teams workshop. Take the ideas you like and use them in your own way.